BOOKWORMS

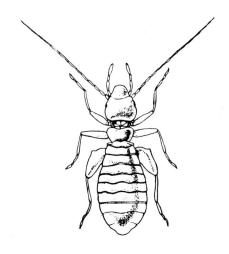

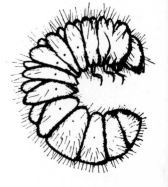

BOOKWORMS

THE INSECT
PESTS OF BOOKS

by

NORMAN HICKIN

Ph.D., F.I.Biol., F.Z.S., F.R.E.S.,

LONDON: SHEPPARD PRESS

Published by
SHEPPARD PRESS LIMITED
Russell Chambers, Covent Garden,
London WC2E 8AX

First edition September 1985

ISBN: 0 900661 38 0

MADE IN ENGLAND
Typeset for the publishers by TRINTYPE
Printed by NENE LITHO
and bound by WOOLNOUGH BOOKBINDING
All of Irthlingborough, Northamptonshire.

CONTENTS

FOREWORD

This book has been written for all who have the responsibility of caring for books, whether as amateurs or professionals; especially it is for those concerned with the conservation of antiquarian books, with collections of books in warm temperate and sub-tropical climates, and with books where recent storage conditions have been less than ideal.

Perhaps some explanation is required for the title. Over the last couple of hundred years the meaning of the word 'worm' has been sharpened. Deriving from the Latin vermis it once signified anything that crept or crawled, and included snakes as well as the larvae of insects (bookworm, silkworm, woodworm) and molluscs (shipworm). Nearly four hundred years ago when, in 1599, Ben Jonson first used the word 'bookworm' in a figurative sense to describe a person he did not like, it is certain that a high proportion of books were infested with bookworms, and they were commonly encountered by all who read books. Today few people have ever seen one, but we are all aware that books, at least old books, are beset by insect pests.

Although we still use the word to describe a person whose head is always buried in a book, we tend now to shy away from the use of such imprecise terms, but it seemed a suitable title for this volume.

Until the last hundred years or so, Europe was a vast repository of printed books many of which were not always maintained as they should have been, but there has been a great shift to North America, and many of the great and important libraries of early books are located there. Without going into details of how they were carried across, we need only say that many insect pests, too, are found on both sides of the Atlantic. Indeed many are encountered in most temperate parts of the world. This work then covers the book pests of Europe and North America, and when appropriate other regions are mentioned also.

When researching into the literature on book conservation there was much less on insect deterioration than I had expected. I therefore thought it would be helpful if I included a chapter on the anatomy of insects so that descriptive text in subsequent chapters can be better understood. I have drawn heavily on my Household Insect Pests (1964 and 1974) for Chapter Two of this present work, and taken the opportunity to clarify a few points and shift emphasis onto aspects of significance.

ACKNOW-LEDGEMENTS

I have a number of acknowledgements to make.
  Firstly I have to go back, almost into history, and thank Professor O. W. Richards of the Imperial College of the University of London who supervised my research into 'The food and water requirements of ptinid beetles'. Who was to imagine for a moment that the insect pests of army biscuits (the field rations of the First World War) would be of importance for ever more as the pests of books? Who would have thought that at the age of seventy-four I would go back to that Ph.D. thesis of over forty years ago? I learnt much from Owain Westmacott Richards and I have always been grateful to him.
  I must thank Robin Edwards for his help: his skill as a taxonomist, and his unrivalled experience of insects in buildings which he made available to me, are much appreciated. My thanks to the Reverend Canon J. R. Fenwick who introduced me to the Worcester Cathedral Library and found for me a volume bored by Death Watch beetle. Robert Hill of the Preservation Service of the British Library and Pamela Gilbert of the British Museum (Natural History) and Entomology Library gave me advice on the literature of 'bookworms'.
  I am grateful also to my friend Dr Siegfried Cymorek of the Bayer Organisation, Krefeld, for his ever ready help, to R. G. Adams of the

8

Ministry of Agriculture Slough Laboratory for his interest and assistance, and to Claude Monet, Paris, for letting me have the French common names of book-injuring insects.

I am indebted to Roger Hartley and Peter Bateman for specimen infested books. Dr Peter Cornwell, Director of Research and Development at Rentokil Limited, who kindly allowed access to statistical information, the Library and Photographic Department and gave permission for histograms to be published. I am grateful for the considerable help given to me by my friend W. M. Johns during the final stages of the book. Finally I want to thank Sheila Price who produced the typescripts from my handwriting. I dot my i's and cross my t's: it is only the other twenty-four characters of the alphabet that require expert elucidation.

N.H.

THE AUTHOR

Norman Ernest Hickin was born at Aston, Birmingham in 1910 and went to the Grammar School there and afterwards to the Central Technical College. He graduated B.Sc. in Zoology with Special Entomology in 1936, and obtained his Ph.D. in 1940 as an external student of the University of London. His thesis was on the ptinidiae, spider beetles well known as pests of old books, so an early start was made on gathering material for the present volume.

Most of Norman Hickin's professional life was spent with Rentokil Limited, the pest control and wood preservation firm, of which he was Technical Manager and Director from 1944 to 1957, Scientific Director from 1957 to 1972, and Scientific Consultant since April 1972. He became known throughout the world as an authority on the wood-boring beetle family ANOBIIDAE, which includes several of the most important pests of books in Europe, and he wrote widely on them, both in popular style and in textbooks. He studied termites, which outside the cold temperate regions are by far the most damaging book pests, in Australia, California, East Africa, Florida, Guyana, Southern France and the West Indies.

Lecturing has taken him to Melbourne, Sydney, and Perth in Australia, Auckland and Wellington in New Zealand, Los Angeles, New York and Purdue in the United States of America, Belgrade, Berlin, Moscow, Prague, Stockholm and Vienna in Europe. He has always believed in communicating to colleagues, friends and students of his subjects, and has written seventeen well-illustrated books. He says he is a bookworm himself.

BOOKWORMS
THE INSECT PESTS OF BOOKS

CHAPTER ONE

INTRODUCTION
TO THE PROBLEM

MATERIALS OF
ORGANIC ORIGIN

Since the beginning of civilisation Man has felt the need to store information for eventual retrieval. The manner in which this has been done and changes in the materials used have marked important stages in his development.

The incising or engraving of stone was perhaps one of the earliest methods employed. Primitive man might perhaps be forgiven for thinking that the marks he made on the rocks would last for ever. Some have, indeed, lasted for centuries, but most have not, as a visit to any English graveyard will confirm.

The great step forward, which was taken more or less simultaneously in the Middle East and in the Far East, was the use of flat sheets of material of organic origin. These were at first the prepared skins of mammals de-haired, stretched and dried on frames, which gave vellum and parchment. Later sheets of vegetable fibre, at first whole plant tissues, then plant cells with thickened walls gave us paper.

From the beginning books, whether in the form of reading rolls or codici (the familiar leaves bound in covers) have been constructed of materials of animal or vegetable origin with, exceptionally, some pigments derived from minerals. It is the organic origin of the materials used in book construction which puts them at hazard to organisms capable of bringing about their decay. This fact should be appreciated by every book conservator: the destruction of books is a natural process, but man has intervened and tried to modify natural substances for his own purposes. In this case to make the written and printed word last longer.

The principal constituent materials of early books are:

LEATHER. An ancient word in many forms, used for animal skins (usually mammals, but occasionally reptiles, and rarely birds or fish, e.g. ostrich or shark) which have been chemically treated with vegetable or mineral substances to render them durable and pliable.

Morocco leather, or simply 'morocco', is leather made from goat skins tanned with sumac, originally made in Morocco, then in the Levant and Turkey, but now in Europe, although the goat skins are still imported from Africa and Asia. There are many imitations which are usually made from sheep or lamb skins.

Tanning is to treat the skins or hides by steeping them in an infusion of an astringent bark, such as that of oak, or some similarly effective process. Tannin was made from oak galls, originally gallotannic acid, but there are many allied substances which have the property of combining with animal hide and converting it into leather.

PARCHMENT is made from the inner skin, usually of sheep or goat but sometimes of other animals, dressed and prepared for writing, painting, etc. There have been many forms of the word, the earliest dating from about the year 1300 when it was 'parchemin'. The name is believed to have been derived from Pergamum, a city in Asia Minor.

VELLUM is a high quality sort of parchment made from the skins of calves or the young of other animals such as lambs or kids. The earliest use of the word seems to have been in 1440, and it appears since in many variants. As well as being used for writing and painting, it was used as a binding material.

PAPER. The first paper of Middle East origin was made from thin sheets of plant tissue from the stem of the Paper Reed or Paper Rush (Cyperus papyrus or Papyrus antiquorum). This large aquatic plant was once abundant in Egypt and now still covers extensive areas in the basin of the Lower Nile. The paper was produced by layering thin slices of the tissue, generally three layers thick, the inner at right angles to the outer layers. It was then soaked in water and dried. The word 'paper' is derived from 'papyrus' but is now used for paper made from cotton, linen and many other fibres. Today paper consists of fibres interlaced into a complex web and rolled out into a thin flexible sheet. Linen, cotton, rags, straw, wood, a number of grass species, and many other fibrous materials have been used by macerating in a mill until a pulp has been formed, when it is pressed, rolled and dried. Other substances may be added at various stages, in order to impart special properties, such as bleaching or colouring agents, size to give gloss or mineral matter to increase weight.

Parchment paper is a tough translucent glossy kind of paper which resembles parchment. Vegetable parchment is also paper resembling parchment. Cotton parchment has the appearance of parchment but is made by soaking cotton fibre in a solution of sulphuric acid and glycerin in water and rolling it into sheets. The word has come to be loosely used for any parchment-like document or manuscript, in many physical forms, whatever the origin. Again we get vellum paper and vegetable vellum. As with parchment the word has been used for imitations, but the material styled 'vellum' must be superior to 'parchment'.

BIODETERIORATION

It is a universal characteristic of organic material, whether derived from animals or plants, that it rots or decays. There is deterioration, a falling away in the original properties associated with the material. This may be in the short term, a few minutes, days, weeks or months, or in the long term perhaps as much as several hundred years.

Man may delay the onset of decay, or biodeterioration as it is now called, in many substances which are of use to him, but the process is inevitable. Several categories of agencies or factors bring this about. Some are physical, mechanical or chemical, and they will not be considered further here, but probably the most important causes of injury or decay to material of organic origin are biological. These are living organisms, either vegetable or animal which have evolved so as to obtain their nourishment and shelter from dead organic matter. Thus, paper, leather, wood, silk, and wool, of which books have been constructed for many centuries often fall victims to bacteria, moulds, mildews (fungi), insects and arthropods. Only the insects and a few non-insect arthropods are discussed in this present work.

CHAPTER TWO

INSECTS AS MEMBERS OF THE ANIMAL KINGDOM

The animal kingdom is first divided into two main groups, those that possess back bones (vertebrates) and those that do not (invertebrates). One of the major invertebrate groups is the ARTHROPODA. The class INSECTA is by far the most important arthropod group to Man.

In this book as the title suggests, we describe the Insects which are known to damage books, together with a few mites of the class ARACHNIDA.

The class ARACHNIDA consists of the spiders, mites and ticks. They differ from other classes of the ARTHROPODA in possessing eight legs in the adult stage. A few mites are implicated in book damage. DIPLOPODA, the millipedes are well-known and are mostly feeders on vegetable material and bear two pairs of legs on most of the segments. The CHILOPODA, the centipedes are predaceous and are characterized by having one pair of legs per segment. Some tropical species are venomous.

INSECTS AS ANIMALS

Insects are animals of the class INSECTA which in turn belong to the large group or *phylum* ARTHROPODA. All members of the group ARTHROPODA have the body divided into segments and the skeleton consists of a hard or horny external covering. This is known as an exo-skeleton. In addition, a number of the body segments bear pairs of appendages which are jointed and which vary in size and shape according to their function and to their position on the body.

The class INSECTA, or Insects, consists of arthropods in which, in the adult stage, the body is divided into three distinct regions: THE HEAD which bears a single pair of antennae, a pair of mandibles and two pairs of mouthparts called maxillae, the second pair of which is fused down the centre; THE THORAX from which arise three pairs of legs and either one or two pairs of wings. In the more primitive insects, however, wings have not been evolved, e.g. the Silverfish *Lepisma saccharina*, and in some highly evolved insects the wings have been lost, e.g. the fleas, *Siphonaptera*; THE ABDOMEN which bears neither walking legs nor wings but a genital opening occurs near the extremity but appendages known as cerci may be present.

Insects may also be differentiated anatomically by their method of breathing. Air is circulated to all regions and organs of the body through a ramification of minute tubes called tracheae (the smallest are called tracheoles) which open to the outside through pores or 'spiracles' situated along the sides of the body.

Other classes in the *phylum* ARTHROPODA are CRUSTACEA containing the crabs, shrimps, lobsters and woodlice.

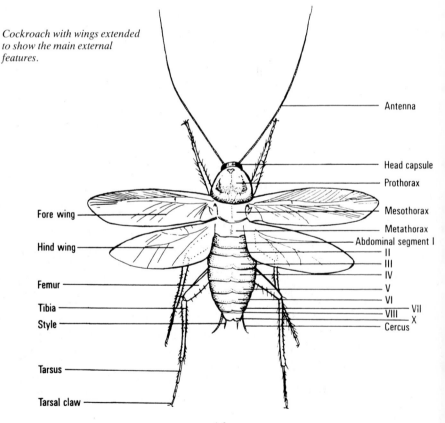

Cockroach with wings extended to show the main external features.

Antenna

Head capsule

Prothorax

Fore wing

Mesothorax

Metathorax

Hind wing

Abdominal segment I

II

III

IV

Femur

V

VI

Tibia

VII

VIII

Style

X

Cercus

Tarsus

Tarsal claw

16

THE SHAPE OF INSECTS

It has been estimated that there are about three and a half million different species of insects living in the world today and of these only about one-fifth have been described and named. In view of the wide range of adaptation and form shown by insects, therefore, if an attempt is to be made to identify insect species, it is essential to understand the general pattern of insect shape and the essential parts of which the body is composed. We have already defined what an insect is by reference to its constituent parts and external and internal organs, so that we will now describe a whole insect, using the cockroach as an example.

THE HEAD is capsule-like and bears at its extremity the mouthparts. These consist of an upper lip, two pairs of jaws (the mandibles and the maxillae) and the lower lip. The maxillae and the lower lip bear segmented tactile organs called palps. Illustrations of the mouthparts of certain insects are given later in the text in the descriptions of certain species of insect pests of books.

THE NECK. The head is joined to the thorax by a small, for the most part, membraneous neck. The sclerotized areas are small, allowing for a certain amount of head movement both to and fro and forwards and backwards.

THE THORAX is composed of three fairly distinct parts:

The *prothorax* bears the first pair of legs and the top surface is shield-shaped.

The *mesothorax* bears the second pair of legs and the first pair of wings (the forewings) modified into horny elytra in the case of beetles.

The *metathorax* bears the third pair of legs and the second pair of wings (the hindwings) folded up under the elytra in the case of beetles.

THE LEGS. The legs of insects consist of a number of articulating parts, and although in some insect species certain of these parts may be

17

reduced or even missing, normally it is posible to refer the legs of insects to a common plan.

Commencing from that part of the leg nearest to the body of the insect it is made up of the following parts:

The *coxa*, which is stout and of fair size.

The *trochanter*, which is usually small.

The *femur*, almost always long and stout.

The *tibia*, which is long and not quite so stout.

The *tarsus*, which consists of five small parts, the last terminating in a pair of claws.

THE SKELETAL SYSTEM OF INSECTS

The skeleton of an insect consists almost entirely of the integument enveloping its body. In most adult insects this integument or body wall is hard, being composed of a number of horny plates connected by an elastic membraneous skin to allow for movement. In other insects and in most larval insects the integument is almost entirely membraneous although the head and jaws may be horny. The skeletal system then, of an insect is entirely integumentary and being the outside layer it is known as the Exoskeleton.

Position of alimentary canal, central nervous system and blood system in a generalized (hypothetical) insect, from the side. Partly after Imms.

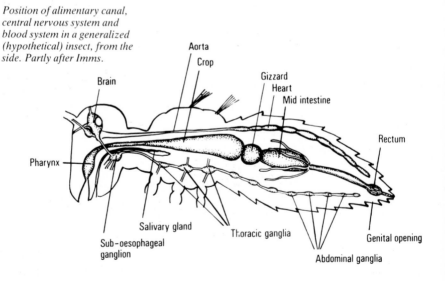

Aorta

Crop

Brain

Gizzard

Heart

Mid intestine

Rectum

Pharynx

Salivary gland

Sub-oesophageal ganglion

Thoracic ganglia

Abdominal ganglia

Genital opening

THE EXOSKELETON

The integument of an insect is built up of several layers, see figure below.

The outer layer or cuticle which shows the following divisions: commencing from the outside these are: the very thin epicuticle which is waxy and helps to prevent water loss; a much thicker exocuticle; and an even thicker laminated endocuticle. These three parts of the cuticle are non-living although complex processes may be elaborated within their structure.

The hypodermis, which is a single layer of cells containing various glands associated with the cuticle, and specialized cells concerned with the moulting process (see later). It is the hypodermis which secretes the cuticle.

The basement membrane is a thin sheet of tissue adherent to the base of the hypodermis. It serves for the attachment of muscles and is also associated wtih blood-cells from which it is thought it might have its origin.

Chemical constitution of the cuticle. Reference has already been made to the horny cuticle of insects. It is usual to refer to the hardening of the cuticular layer of insects as 'sclerotization'. It is of interest to note the chemical materials of which it is constituted. In the main two substances are associated together. These are chitin and protein and both contain nitrogen as well as carbon, hydrogen and oxygen. Chitin is a relatively stable substance being unaffected by water, alkalis, dilute acids or organic solvents.

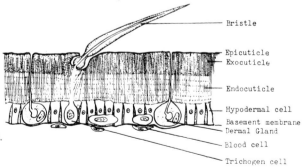

Section of typical insect cuticle. Highly magnified. (After Wigglesworth)

Bristle
Epicuticle
Exocuticle
Endocuticle
Hypodermal cell
Basement membrane
Dermal Gland
Blood cell
Trichogen cell

THE RESPIRATORY SYSTEM OF AN INSECT

In almost all insects, respiration, or gas exchange, takes place by means of a complex system of internal air-tubes which are known as tracheae. Air enters the body of the insect through small openings known as spiracles arranged in a series along both sides of the body. By means of the tracheae and the small tracheoles air is then conveyed directly to all parts of the body and the appendages. The aquatic larvae of some insects are furnished with gills, but this type of respiration is exceptional.

THE FUNCTION OF THE SPIRACLE

This is to provide an opening for air to enter the tracheal system, to restrict the entrance of deleterious substances and at the same time prevent water loss.

THE NUMBER OF SPIRACLES

The number of spiracles present in insects varies greatly. In one type of arrangement there are two pairs present in the thorax and eight pairs in the abdomen. Other types of spiracle arrangements appear to have been derived from this pattern by one or more pairs becoming non-functional. In the larvae of some species of two-winged flies there is a pair of spiracles present only in the prothorax and the last segment of the abdomen. In the larvae of some other species of two-winged flies, on the other hand, spiracles are present only on the last abdominal segment. This great reduction in the number of functional spiracles is said to be an adaptation to life in water or a liquid medium.

THE SPIRACLE STRUCTURE

Essentially, a spiracle consists of a horny margin leading to a vestibule which may be hairy or spiny to prevent the entrance of dust. It is provided with muscles which can close the spiracular entrance under certain conditions, such as when water loss may be excessive. Sometimes glands are present which by secreting a water-repellent substance prevent the spiracle from getting wet, which would otherwise fill or clog with water and thus prevent the ingress of air.

When an insect is being dissected, the tracheal tubes may be identified by their silvery appearance due to the contained air. When highly magnified under the microscope the tracheal tube has a striated appearance. This has a spring-like action keeping the tracheae open and fully distended. The smallest tubes, the tracheoles, have a similar although much smaller structure. The diameter of the tracheoles is only about $\frac{1}{5,000}$ of a millimetre!

The ends of the tracheoles may join up with other tracheoles to form a minute, delicate reticulated network over the surface of an organ or piece of tissue, or they may end inside the actual cells of muscle and other tissue.

In addition to the tracheae, many winged insects contain air-sacs which are special dilated thin-walled tracheae. The air-sacs act as a reservoir, increasing the amount of available air in the body of the insect, and, in addition, lower the specific gravity of the insect. This is, of course, a great advantage in flight.

RESPIRATION Oxygen travels through the tracheole walls inwards and carbon dioxide outwards by diffusion. The amount of carbon dioxide is less than the amount of oxygen used for respiration. It is also so much more permeable than oxygen that a substantial amount is lost through the general body surface of the insect and does not require to be specially expelled from the tracheal contents.

When the insect is walking or flying there is sufficient dilation and contraction of the tracheal system by muscular movement for the additional oxygen required to be drawn in through the spiracles.

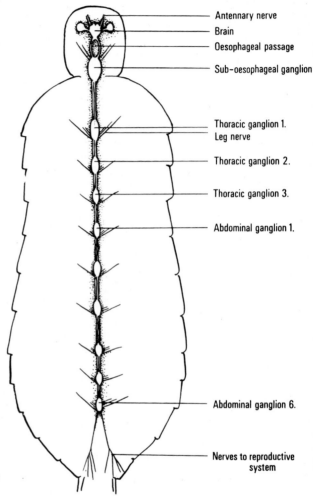

Antennary nerve
Brain
Oesophageal passage
Sub-oesophageal ganglion

Thoracic ganglion 1.
Leg nerve

Thoracic ganglion 2.

Thoracic ganglion 3.

Abdominal ganglion 1.

Abdominal ganglion 6.

Nerves to reproductive system

Central nervous system of the Cockroach from above.

THE NERVOUS SYSTEM OF AN INSECT

In all animals the nervous system is a connecting link between all the organs of sense, that is, all the organs which respond to the various sorts of stimuli such as light, touch, smell, taste, etc., and the muscles and glands. Nervous tissue is essentially composed of neurones or nerve-cells in a general supporting tissue. The nerve-cell usually bears a number of long filaments which enable it to maintain contact, either directly or in a series with other nerve-cells, between the sense organ and the 'effecting' organ, such as a muscle or a gland. Long conducting nerve-fibres are composed of a number of nerve-cells grouped together as nervous centres or ganglia (singular, ganglion).

The nervous system of an insect is divided into three parts as follows:

THE CENTRAL NERVOUS SYSTEM

This is the most important part of the nervous system and is composed of a series of ganglia united in pairs sometimes so closely that they appear as one, and they are united by long nerve-fibre strands called connectives. The central nervous system of the Cockroach is shown opposite.

THE BRAIN. In a typical insect, there is a pair of ganglia in each segment of the body but often adjacent pairs may coalesce. This latter condition occurs in the head where the brain consists of three distinct but fused ganglia-masses. The largest part of the brain and also that part which innervates the eyes is the first part of the ganglia-masses. They are called the optic lobes and optic ganglia. It is of interest to note that those insects with large compound eyes have correspondingly large optic lobes and optic ganglia. The second part of the brain innervates the antennae and the swellings which are a feature of this part are known as the olfactory lobes.

THE SUBOESOPHAGEAL GANGLION. The oesophagus or throat lies immediately under the brain and

23

beneath this lies a double ganglion called the suboesophageal ganglion. Connectives join this ganglion to the brain by encircling the throat. This ganglion innervates the mouthparts and the lower part of the head.

THE VENTRAL NERVE-CORD. The remainder of the central nervous system consists of a series of paired ganglia lying on the floor of the thorax and abdomen which constitutes the ventral nerve-cord. The first three pairs of ganglia are situated in the thorax and innervate the legs and the latter two pairs the wings also. The number of ganglia in the abdomen varies greatly in different insects. Often the first abdominal ganglia coalesce with the last thoracic ganglia.

THE VISCERAL NERVOUS SYSTEM

This is a series of three sympathetic nervous systems, the first of which innervates, principally, the intestine and heart. The second system innervates the spiracles, that is the outer openings of the tracheal system. The third system arises from the last ganglion of the abdominal nerve-cord. It innervates the reproductive system and the hinder part of the alimentary canal.

THE PERIPHERAL NERVOUS SYSTEM

This system consists mainly of a delicate ramification of nerve-cells innervating many organs and sensory hairs and bristles arising from the integument and thus occurs just beneath the latter. In addition, part of this system is to be found on the wall of the alimentary canal. The peripheral nervous system arises from the central nervous system.

THE BLOOD OR VASCULAR SYSTEM OF AN INSECT

In an insect, circulation of blood takes place in open cavities of the body system which includes also cavities in all the appendages, such as legs and antennae. There is only one closed blood-vessel. This consists of a long tube known as the dorsal vessel which lies immediately beneath the integument at the top or dorsal surface of the

24

insect in the middle line. The front part, which commences behind the brain and traverses the thorax, is thin, and is called the aorta. The hinder part which traverses the whole of the abdomen, is segmented in relation to the segments of the abdomen and is wider than the aorta and is known as the heart. In each segment is a pair of slit-like openings which allow blood to enter and is there pumped forwards to the aorta which is the main artery.

The blood of insects consists of liquid plasma and blood-cells or haemocytes. It freely bathes the internal organs and appendages. The blood-cells store and transport food substances and the plasma is the main storage of water. The blood also carries hormones around the body and also has a mechanical function in such actions as expansion of wings as, for example, in butterflies and moths. It should be noted that in the blood of insects the transport of oxygen is of relatively little importance, on account of the extensive and efficient development of the tracheal system.

THE ALIMENTARY CANAL OF AN INSECT

The alimentary canal of insects is a fairly simple tube having its origin at the mouth and ending at the anus at the hinder end of the abdomen. The alimentary canal of the Cockroach is shown on page 26. In some insects it is straight but in others it is long enough to be thrown into a series of folds. The alimentary canal is divided into three main parts according to its embryonic origin.

THE FORE INTESTINE: This originates as a pushing-in of the integument in the mouth region. From the mouth, the pharynx leads backwards to the oesophagus which occupies the fore part of the thorax. The inner walls of the oesophagus are folded lengthways. The hinder part of the oesophagus is usually enlarged as a crop and its function is to store food. The last part of the fore intestine consists of a pear-shaped gizzard, sometimes called the proventriculus. Its walls are thick and muscular and there are many tooth-like projections from the inner wall for breaking up food. There is often a valve at the point of junction between the fore and mid-intestine which prevents food from passing forward from the mid- to the fore intestine.

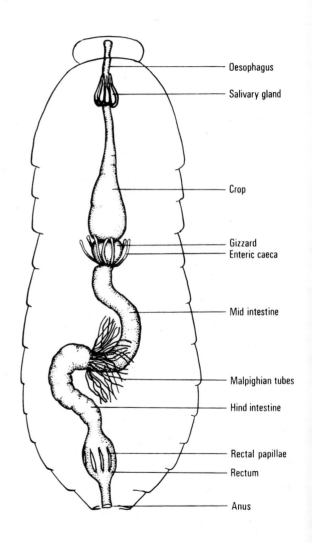

Oesophagus

Salivary gland

Crop

Gizzard
Enteric caeca

Mid intestine

Malpighian tubes

Hind intestine

Rectal papillae

Rectum

Anus

Alimentary canal of the Cockroach. Partly diagrammatic dissection from above.

THE MID-INTESTINE: This is also called the mid-gut or stomach. It is sometimes bag-like, sometimes thin and looped or coiled. In the Cockroach there are a number of finger-like processes arising from the junction of the fore and mid-intestine called enteric caeca, which increase the inner wall area. In other insects they may be more numerous, fewer, or absent altogether. In some larvae which feed on liquid matter, the mid-intestine is a closed sac as when the nutrient material has been absorbed by the epithelial layer of the mid-intestine, there is little or nothing left as a solid residue.

THE HIND INTESTINE: It is usual for the hind intestine of most insects to show three distinct regions as follows:

The small intestine, or ileum, the junction of which with the mid-intestine is normally shown by the presence of the pyloric valve and a number of thin hair-like tubes known as the Malpighian tubes (named after their discoverer, the Italian Malphigi).

The large intestine or colon from which, in moths and beetles, arises a hollow outgrowth or caecum.

The rectum is more or less globular or pear-shaped and bears on the inside a number of knob-like protrusions which have been called rectal glands. Their function is said to be the absorption of water from faecal matter. Water loss in an insect is a very important hazard and these rectal glands are one means of minimizing it. It is thought also that inorganic salts soluble in water may also be absorbed at this point.

THE REPRODUCTIVE SYSTEM OF AN INSECT

A wide range of structure and shape is found in insects but it is of interest to note that the embryonic appearance of both male and female systems is similar. The organs of reproduction are situated wholly in the abdomen and generally in the hinder part. The genital openings occur in the under-side of the abdomen. In the case of males, the penis is everted from a position normally behind the ninth abdominal segment, and in the case of females the genital opening lies on or behind the eighth or ninth segment.

MALE REPRODUCTIVE SYSTEM consists of the following organs:

1. The *testes* (singular is testis) are paired and consist of a number of testicular tubes or follicles. They may be situated either above, below or at the sides of the alimentary canal. The spermatozoa are produced by special zones of tissues in the testes and are released into the *vasa deferentia*.

2. The *vasa deferentia* (singular is vas deferens) are paired tubes leading from the testes to a reservoir (the vesicula seminalis) in which the spermatozoa are stored.

3. The *vesicula seminalis* may be a common receptacle or it may be paired (plural is vesiculae seminales).

4. The *single ejaculatory duct* leads from the vesiculae seminales to the external opening. It is strongly muscular and part of the organ may be everted to form the terminal aedeagus.

5. The *accessory glands* are special glands from one to three pairs in number associated with the male genital system. The secretions of these glands may mix with the spermatozoa or may, in appropriate cases, take part in the formation of spermatophores.

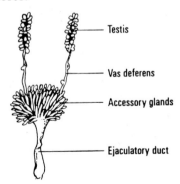

Testis

Vas deferens

Accessory glands

Ejaculatory duct

Male reproductive system of the Cockroach.

28

FEMALE REPRODUCTIVE SYSTEM consists of the following organs:

1. The *ovaries*. There are two ovaries which lie on each side of the alimentary canal. Each ovary is made up of a number of tubes called ovarioles in which the eggs develop. At the apex of each ovariole is a terminal filament. All the filaments of each ovary join togeher before joining with the joined filaments of the ovary on the opposite side. At the apex of each ovariole is sited the tissue in which the germ-cells have their origin. As the germ-cells develop they pass down the ovariole tube towards the oviduct, being nourished by the special cells in the wall of the ovariole, and finally receive their skins and shells before being passed into the common oviduct.

2. *Common oviduct*. This is a muscular tube from the paired oviducts to the vagina.

3. The *vagina*. This consists of a shallow chamber arising from the hinder part of the eighth abdominal segment. In some insects there is a pouch-like extension known as the *bursa copulatrix*. It is of interest to note here that in the Common Furniture Beetle, *Anobium punctatum*, a pair of pouches arise from the vagina containing symbiotic yeasts which become attached to the eggs as they are laid. Thus, when the hatching larva emerges from the shell by consuming a part of it, the yeast-cells are transferred to its gut. The yeast-cells play an important part in the digestion of cellulose.

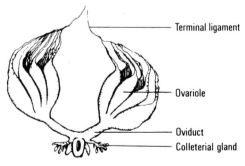

Female reproductive system of the Cockroach.

Terminal ligament

Ovariole

Oviduct

Colleterial gland

29

4. The *spermatheca* is also known as the *receptaculum seminis*. It arises as a pouch or duct from the vagina and serves to receive the spermatozoa and to store them until the developing eggs are in the condition for fertilization.

5. The *accessory glands*. These are known also as *collaterial glands*, of which there may be one or two pairs. They arise from the vagina and secrete substances associated with the eggs, such as the material for the egg-pod in Cockroaches and the cement enabling the eggs to adhere together in some other insects. The poison-glands of the wasps are special adaptations of the colleterial glands.

REPRODUCTION

Reproduction in insects is carried out by a typical sexual process whereby the male inserts the penis into the genital system of the female, via the vagina, and transfers spermatozoa. The latter are stored either by themselves or in a coherent body (a spermatophore) from which they escape. A spermatozoon fuses with an egg-cell to fertilize it and subsequently the egg is laid.

There are exceptions to this process. In some insects reproduction can take place without fertilization of the eggs by spermatozoa. This is known as *Parthenogenesis* and may occur periodically as a regular feature of the life-cycle or it may take place only occasionally and intermittently. In some insects more than one individual can develop from a single egg. This is called *Polyembryony*. A few insects are viviparous, most usually they produce living larvae direct from the vagina, the eggs having been retained within the oviduct or vagina to the hatching stage. Examples are known, however, in which pre-pupae, adults, or nymphs are produced by the adult female.

THE INSECT ORDERS

The natural orders in which insects are placed usually give little difficulty to the students of insect life as most would be able to recognize a beetle (COLEOPTERA), a two-winged fly (DIPTERA), a butterfly or moth (LEPIDOPTERA) and some of the other more important insect orders.

A Synopsis of the more important Insect Orders with special attention given to those orders containing Insects which cause injury to books.

Some orders of no significance have been omitted.

APTERYGOTA

(Primitively wingless)

Order 1. Bristletails (THYSANURA). Mouthparts for biting. Body clothed with scales. Abdomen terminating in cerci (a cercus is an abdominal appendage) and a median filament. Body generally carrot-shaped. The Silverfish belongs to this group.

Order 4. Springtails (COLLEMBOLA). Mouthparts for biting. Abdomen with leaping appendage. Some species found in very damp situations indoors.

PTERYGOTA
EXOPTERYGOTA

(winged insects)

(wings developing externally)

Order 9. Grasshoppers, Locusts and Crickets (ORTHOPTERA). Forewings leathery. Mouthparts for biting. Female generally with well-developed ovipositor. Hind legs large and well-developed for jumping.

Order 11. Earwigs (DERMAPTERA). Mouthparts for biting. Forewings small and leathery, hindwings large and membraneous, folded beneath forewings when at rest. Abdomen terminates in forceps.

Order 13. Cockroaches and Mantids (DICTYOPTERA). Legs for running, cerci segmented, forewings leathery, ovipositor concealed. Eggs are laid in pouch-like cases. Long filamentous antennae.

Order 14. Termites (ISOPTERA). Mouthparts for biting. Both pairs of wings similar or they may be

31

absent. In wingless forms, eyes are also absent. Social insects living in communities of greater or lesser complexity. No British species, but a great economic importance in tropical and subtropical countries. A number of species injurious to books.

Order 16. Book Lice or Psocids (PSOCOPTERA). Mouthparts for biting. Wings membraneous with reduction in veins. Very small insects. Antennae long, many-jointed. Some species associated with book damage.

Order 17. Biting Lice (MALLOPHAGA). Mouthparts for biting. Most species found on birds where they feed on pieces of skin and feathers. Wings absent. Eyes reduced.

Order 18. Sucking Lice (ANOPLURA). Mouthparts for piercing and sucking. Found only on mammals on which they feed by puncturing the skin and sucking blood. Wings absent. Eyes reduced. The body and head louse are in this order.

Order 19. Plant Bugs, Frog Hoppers, Aphids, Scale Insects, Water Scorpions, Water Boatmen (HEMIPTERA). Mouthparts for piercing and sucking. Wings with few veins and either forewings leathery or basal half-leathery. Includes the Bed Bug.

Order 20. Thrips (THYSANOPTERA). Small insects with specialized mouthparts to break the tissues of plants and suck the sap. Wings long and narrow, fringed with long hairs. Often enter houses fortuitously in vast numbers. Often found dead in the leaves of books but cause no damage, and can sometiems be found in framed pictures where their small size has enabled them to enter cracks.

ENDOPTERYGOTA (wings developing internally)

Order 21. The Lacewings (NEUROPTERA). Mouthparts for sucking in larvae, biting in adults. Wings membraneous with many cross-veins. Predacious larvae. Some species hibernate in buildings but cause no direct damage.

32

Order 23. Butterflies and Moths (LEPIDOPTERA). Larval mouthparts for biting. In adults, mouthparts modified into a long coiled tube, and mandibles absent. Wings covered with scales, often brightly coloured. Several moth species can damage books.

Order 25. Two-winged Flies (DIPTERA). Highly modified mouthparts for biting in larvae and sucking or piercing and sucking in adults. Forewings membraneous, hindwings minute, modified as balancing organs. Larvae are legless.

Order 26. The Fleas (SIPHONAPTERA). Small insects, wingless and laterally compressed. Eyes always simple if present. Antennae short and stout, reposing in grooves. Mouthparts for piercing and sucking. Larvae are legless. Adults are parasitic on warm-blooded animals.

Order 27. Ants, Bees, Sawflies, Ichneumon Flies, etc. (HYMENOPTERA). Mouthparts for biting or sucking in adults and for biting in most larvae. Two pairs of membraneous wings, forewings larger and linked by a row of hooks to fore-edge of hindwing. First abdominal segment fused with thorax. Ovipositor often modified for sawing, piercing or stinging.

Order 28. Beetles (COLEOPTERA). Mouthparts for biting in larvae and adults, for biting and sucking in some larvae. Forewings modified as hard leathery covers (elytra) for membraneous functional hindwings. Wings have few veins. The largest order in the animal kingdom, of which there are a quarter of a million described species. About 3,700 species are found in the British Isles. Three families, DERMESTIDAE, ANOBIIDAE and PTINIDAE, contain important book-damaging species.

HOW INSECTS ARE CLASSIFIED

The broad divisions into which the class INSECTA is divided have now been described as far as the insect Order and the main characteristics of the principal insect Orders have been given. We shall now see how the orders of insects are subdivided.

The insect Order is divided into a number of primary divisions called suborders, which in turn divided into groups called families. Suborders are often confusing to the non-entomologist and have been omitted in this present account. It is usual for the name of the insect family to end in – IDAE, for example the name of the family of the LEPIDOPTERA, to which the Common Clothes Moth *Tineola bisselliella* belongs, is the TINAEIDAE. In many cases, but not all, the families are divided into subfamilies, in which case it is usual for the name to end in – INAE. Again subfamilies have been omitted as they are of significance only to entomological specialists. In all cases, however, the families or subfamiies are divided into the smallest groups known as genera (singular is genus). Each genus is made up of one or more distinct kinds known as species.

It must be emphasized that the classification of insects is a natural one, insects being classified in the way that they have evolved, closely related species being placed together. The closest relationship is thus the genus, then the subfamily and then the family.

HOW INSECTS ARE NAMED

It will have been observed that the scientific name of an insect consists of two words. The first word of the name is the name of the genus, that is, the smallest group of related species, and it is spelt with an initial capital letter. The second word of the name is the name of the species and it is always spelt with a small letter. In manuscript and typescript both words are underlined to signify that they would appear in italics when printed. The name given to a genus is never duplicated although this may be so in the case of specific names, but never in the same genus. Thus the combination of the generic name and the individual specific name can only mean one particular species and, furthermore, its relationship with a group of species can be seen at once. More correctly, the name of the author who first described and named the insect, according to the Linnaean system described above, should follow the name either in full or in abbreviated form, but this rule need not be adopted on every occasion.

Linnaeus 1707-78 was the founder of the modern system of naming animals (and plants too) and it is named after him. It originated with the publication of the tenth edition of his *Systema Naturae* in 1758. It has been universally adopted and it has enabled the naming of insects to be conducted in an exact manner. That is not to say that complications and anomalies never arise, but, taken generally, the system works well.

The law of Priority prevails; the first name accompanied by an adequate description, to be put forward after 1758 is accepted subject to a few minor rules. In exceptional cases the International Commission for Zoological Nomenclature may bend the rules if confusion is likely to arise but their decision is accepted.

HOW INSECTS EVOLVED

The first or oldest insects known from fossil records occurred in the Devonian period. They were wingless and are known as the APTERYGOTA and were rather like the modern Springtails (COLLEMBOLA). They are mentioned and illustrated in this book because they are indicative of very damp situations in buildings. The number of species in the four orders of these primitively wingless insects is very small compared with the vast numbers of species in about 28 orders of winged insects. We should mention here however some wingless insects (such as Fleas APHANIPTERA) have clearly been evolved from winged insects.

The winged insects are known as the *Pterygota* and their fossil record starts in the upper carboniferous strata. The older orders in this group show that the development of the wings during the life cycle takes place externally. In addition the newly-hatched young are similar in shape to the parents with the exception of size, reproductive organs and possession of wings. This group is known as the EXOPTERYGOTA or HEMIMETABOLA. Examples are Termites, ISOPTERA and Psocids, PSOCOPTERA.

The more highly developed insects show an internal development of the wings and there is a distinct metamorphosis in the immature stages involving a larval and a pupal stage. This group is called the ENDOPTERYGOTA or HOLOMETABOLA. Examples are Moths, LEPIDOPTERA and Beetles, COLEOPTERA.

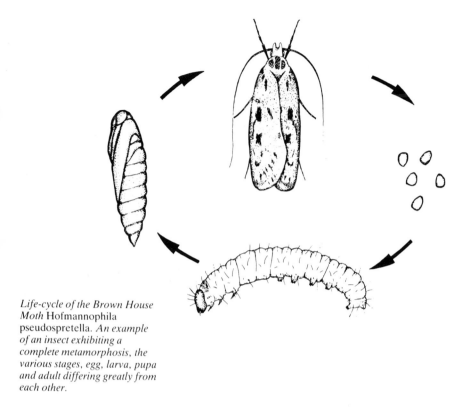

Life-cycle of the Brown House Moth Hofmannophila pseudospretella. *An example of an insect exhibiting a complete metamorphosis, the various stages, egg, larva, pupa and adult differing greatly from each other.*

CHAPTER THREE

THYSANURA
Bristle-tails

This order comprises the most primitive of all insects. The three thoracic segments each bear a pair of small legs. The mouthparts are adapted for biting and the antennae are long and many-segmented. The abdomen consists of eleven segments and terminates with three long segmented bristle-like processes, one central and two lateral and additionally there is a small number of rod-like appendages arising from the hinder end. The general shape of a bristle-tail is generally given as 'carrot-shaped', widest at the thorax and then tapering gradually to the hinder end. Altogether, throughout the world, about 350 species are known but relatively few are associated with man in his buildings. Most spend much of their time concealed amongst rotting leaves and wood but some are to be found only in the nests of social insects such as ants and termites. They are not usually found amongst living herbage. Bristle-tails are generally small but several species reach about 20mm and in colour they are whitish, grey or brownish.

A number of species are covered with scales which give a metallic sheen to the body often described as 'gun metal' or 'silver' and hence 'Silver fish' – almost a universal name not only to a single cosmopolitan species but to a number of others.

A characteristic of the THYSANURA is that wings are never developed and it is this feature that associates them with the primitive insect condition although some entomologists have argued that they are therefore not insects! A metamorphosis is also absent. The immature stages cannot be clearly differentiated, there is only a gradual transition to the adult stage. Indeed, in a number of species of THYSANURA moulting occurs even after eggs have been laid.

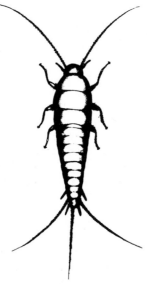

Silverfish. Carrot-shaped. Long antennae, long abdominal appendages and silvery sheen. Wings absent. About 12mm in length.

THE SILVERFISH

Latin: *Lepisma saccharina*
American: *Silverfish*
French: *Lepisme, Lepisme saccharin, Petit poisson d'argent*
German: *Silberfischen*
Spanish: *Pececillo plateado*

Description of Adult Stage

The length of body is 11mm and the long whip-like antennae are about two-thirds of the body length. It is widest at the third thoracic segment then tapers gradually to the end of the abdomen. There are three, long, segmented processes at the end of the abdomen and a number of small unsegmented appendages (the styles). It has a silvery appearance due to the presence of a covering of flat scales. The legs are short but it can turn and twist about and move with great speed hence name of 'Silverfish'. Compound eyes are present each with twelve facets. The mouthparts are simple and undifferentiated and are not unlike those of the cockroach.

Distribution

Widespread and cosmopolitan, it is found throughout Europe, Asia, North America, Australia and New Zealand. In North America it is said to be most common in the eastern states and in the more temperate areas it is not so active in the winter months. It usually occurs in the warmer but more humid parts of a building and hides during daylight amongst paper and similar material but it is often trapped in baths and washbasins. Distribution is thought to be effected by the transport of household goods and foodstuffs.

Time of Emergence

The adult stage ocurs throughout the year.

Feeding Habits

It is thought that carbohydrate materials constitute an important part of this insect's diet. This accounts for the presence of silverfish on books where they feed on starch paste and dextrin as well as the cellulose of paper. Chemically-pulped paper is more often attacked than that mechanically pulped. However, protein-containing substances used in bookbinding such as size, glue and gum are also eaten and books so injured often fall apart when handled. Cellulose-digesting bacteria have been found in the gut of Silverfish.

Busvine quotes Robert Hooke (1665) 'small silver-coloured bookworm . . . supposed to be that which corrodes and eats holes and covers of Books; it appears to the naked eye as a glistening Pearl-coloured Moth; which upon the removing of Books and Papers in the Summer is observed nimbly to scud and pack away to some lurking cranney where it may the better protect itself from appearing dangers'.

Type of Damage to Books	There is a general grazing effect on the surface of materials produced by the scraping of the mandibles. The glazing of paper and other materials is often removed. Paper is often bitten completely through leaving an irregular contour to the edges of paper and usually characterized by the presence of small hemispherical-bitten areas one to two mm in diameter.
Length of Life Cycle	This is recorded by several authorities as being two or three years but on the other hand Sweetman (1938) states that there may be several generations in a year. A difficulty occurs in assessment of this period due to the primitive nature of this species which is able to moult consecutively after laying eggs. There is a problem in determining when the adult stage has been reached as eggs are laid then a moult takes place then eggs are laid again followed by another moult and this is repeated a number of times.
Immature Stages	EGG. The total number of eggs laid may be nearly 200 but the average is probably only about 50. Each batch of eggs must be fertilized by a male. The eggs are broadly oval and measure about 1.5

x 1.0mm. Smooth and whitish at first then yellow then they soon become brownish, shrunken and wrinkled. They may be laid singly or in batches of two or three, at irregular intervals and in cracks, under various objects or dropped quite haphazardly. The incubation period ranges from 43 days at 72°F (22°C) to 19 days at 90°F (32°C).

NYMPHAL STAGE. When newly hatched the young nymph is 2mm in length and white in colour. It is comparatively plumper than the older nymph and is said to be less active. It has a naked apearance bearing neither bristles nor scales. None of the small abdominal appendages, the styles, are present. It is only after the third moult that these appear. They continue to moult throughout their life even after egg-laying has occurred. Associated with this is the ability to regenerate lost limbs at any period of their life cycle.

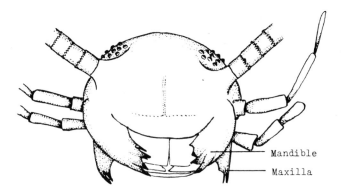

Head of Silverfish. Lepisma saccharina *from the front showing the two pairs of jaw-like mouthparts.*

THE FIREBRAT

Latin: *Lepismodes inquilinus* Newm. but universally known as *Thermobia domestica* Pack.

American: *Firebrat*

French: *Thermobie du boulanger, Marmot du feu Lepisme, Poisson d'argent*

German: *Ofenfischen*

Spanish: *Insecto del fuego*

Description of Adult Stage

The length of body is about 11mm and the antennae are as long as, or longer than the body. It is much wider than the Silverfish and is generally a much stouter insect. It is also different in colour being greyish with dark markings principally on the thoracic segments. It is much more bristly than the Silverfish. It differs also from the Silverfish in having the larger hairs of the dorsal surface on the body being localized into groups (known as combs) at the hinder edge of the tergites whereas on Silverfish they are evenly distributed.

The Firebrat is found in much warmer situations than the Silverfish and although said to be relatively indifferent to the presence of moisture the present author has found it to be abundant in conduit channels in industrial premises where escaping steam rendered the atmosphere very humid.

Distribution

This species and the Silverfish are the only two Bristletails likely to be found in buildings in Britain. It is abundant in suitable localities in the U.S.A. and Canada but although usually referred to as a cosmopolitan insect its distribution is not nearly so wide as the Silverfish. It is mentioned among the pests of Australia. Its place however appears to be taken by the species, *Ctenolepisma longicaudata* Esch. another member of the LEPISMATIDAE.

Time of Emergence

The adult stage occurs throughout the year.

Feeding Habits	This is made up mainly of carbohydrate materials with only a small proportion of protein substances. In bakeries and kitchens, crumbs and flour dust are eaten, in industrial premises the remains and debris from lunch sandwiches often probably moved by pest rodents into inaccessible channels. Wherever this species is found, however it is known to remove the glazing from the surface of paper.
Type of Damage to Books	It is not known specifically as a pest of boks in Britain but in the United States it is recorded as injuring paper and paper products such as books with a glazed finish as mentioned above. This is likely to be in situations where its optimum temperature of 90° to 1067F (32°-41°C). prevails.

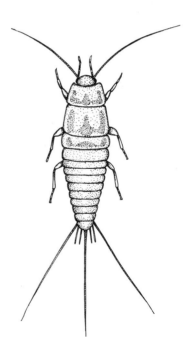

Firebrat Thermobia domestica.
A Bristle-tail found only in warm or hot conditions not necessarily humid but often where there is steam central heating. Pattern of thoracic segments. Excluding appendages 10mm.

Length of Life Cycle	There is difficulty in assessing this as in Silverfish but under optimum conditions lengths of from two months have been recorded and there may be several generations in a year. Another experimenter noted that at 96.8°F (36°C) the length of time from egg to egg is 11 to 12 weeks.
Immature Stages	EGG. Copulation does not take place but after a courtship dance the male drops a sperm bundle which is picked up by the female. The eggs are about 1.0mm in length and 0.7mm in width and are white and opaque. up to about 200 eggs are laid by each female but average about 50. Under optimum conditions incubation takes about twelve days. NYMPHAL STAGE. Hatching takes place with the aid of an egg-burster situated at the front of the head. The young nymph is white and no scales or styles are present and it is sluggish. Only a few days are spent in each of the first four instars, thereafter the duration of each instar is longer. As in the Silverfish a batch of eggs is laid between successive moults which may be as many as 60 and injured limbs are regenerated.

	Latin: *Ctenolepisma longicaudata* Esch.
Description of Adults Stage	This insect has a silvery sheen but immediately becomes darker and assumes a 'gunmetal' shade after moulting. A large 'silverfish' reaching 18mm covered with silvery scales.
Distribution	The midwest and the southern United States. It is also an important pest in southern California where it has been known as *Ctenolepisma urbana* Sla. It has been introduced into Sydney, Australia.
Length of Life Cycle	Sexual maturity is reached in two or three years.

44

Immature Stages

EGG In Australia the eggs are laid in warmer Spring and Summer months in batches of from 2 to 20. Each female lays from 50 to 60 eggs in any one year and they hatch in 3-7 weeks.
NYMPH. The nymphal stage occupies two and a half years and have been known to lay eggs for periods exceeding four years. The adults have been known to survive up to nine months without food.

Latin: *Ctenolepisma campbelli* Barnhart, is a species recorded as damaging book covers in Columbus, Ohio, U.S.A. The name is however open to doubt as a new species, but is recorded also from Australia.

FOUR-LINED SILVERFISH

Latin: *Ctenolepisma quadriseriata* Pack.

Description of Adult Stage

About 15mm in length. Easily recognized by four dark lines extending along the length of the body.

Distribution

California, Oklahoma and New England.

Feeding Habits

It is said to damage fabrics and paper to a greater extent than the Silverfish and Firebrat.

45

CHAPTER FOUR
ISOPTERA
TERMITES

Drywood termites, dampwood termites, subterranean termites.

ISOPTERA means 'equal winged' on account of the sexually mature adults having two pairs of wings of broadly similar size and shape. ISOPTERA undergo a simple metamorphosis – there is no distinct larval and pupal stage. The immature stages generally resemble the adults except that they do not possess wings. In those individuals that are destined to possess wings, they develop externally being clearly visible in the later immature individuals as two pairs of 'wing pads'. It is of interest that the oldest fossil of a termite is a wing from the mid-Permian deposits in the Urals. It is nearly two hundred million years old. Thus they lived before there were flowering plants, butterflies, bees or birds on the earth. Termites are social insects, always living in communities. These may be complex numbering several million individuals or they may be comparatively simple, the community consisting of a few dozen individuals only. Social communities of anything like the same order of complexity as in the termites are found only in the insect order HYMENOPTERA (Ants, bees, wasps).

Geographical
Distribution

Termites are exceedingly abundant, they are found throughout the tropical and subtropical areas of the world and in some areas extending into the temperate regions. Two Species, *Reticulitermes lucifugus* and *Kalotermes flavicollis*, are found in Europe but they do not appear to thrive further north than Paris in France, except that a third species, *Reticulitermes flavipes*, a few colonies of an introduced termite maintained themselves in the basement of warehouses in Hamburg, Germany for a number of years.

Nutrition

Little is known about the nutrition of termites. Considering the importance of termites in the biodeterioration of a host of natural and synthetic substances there is much to be done in this field. Termites subsist on vegetable material almost exclusively although extensive damage is often caused to a host of other materials in the efforts of termites to find cellulosic substances. Damage to plastic material has been recorded on a number of occasions, giving the impression that no useful purpose to the termite colony could have been served. The only animal matter consumed would appear to be the dead bodies of members of the colony. This provides a useful source of protein. Some termites (the drywood species in general) live only in wood and are able to digest cellulose through the agency of colonies of PROTOZOA (primitive unicellular animals) in the intestine. The PROTOZOA secrete the enzyme cellulase which breaks down the cellulose into simpler carbohydrate substances capable of being digested by the termites. Such a relationship, where two dissimilar organisms are intimately associated together for their mutual benefit, is known as symbiosis.

Some subterranean termites, on the other, gather cellulosic material, chew it up and allow fungi to grow in it. This is generally known as a 'fungus garden'. Although the exact process is not clear it would appear that the termites browse on the nodules of hyphae as they appear, much like a mushroom bed. But one of the most interesting features of termite nutrition is the habit of passing food from one individual to another by way of the mouth or by the anus. A high proportion of the nutritional material appears to be extracted from the foodstuff before it is finally discarded and even the excrement is used as a constituent of the very hard cement used in making the termite nest.

Termites live under conditions of static humidity controlled by the use of closed tubes or closed compartments in which the termites live. In this way the termites are able to allow more or less

47

water vapour from the atmosphere to enter the living space. When conditions outside are very hot the termites enter compartments very deep in the ground but when there is not much sun they often inhabit the outer compartments so that every bit of warmth can be obtained from the sunlight. In a number of species the alignment of the 'mound' with regard to the meridian is believed to favour such an arrangement.

CASTES

Queen

Queen Termite

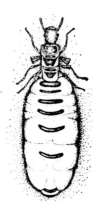

Termites are outstanding amongst insects in that they are divided into a number of different castes or morphologically and functionally different forms. This phenomenon is displayed in the termites with much greater emphasis than in the order HYMENOPTERA (Ants, Bees and Wasps). In due season termites swarm by producing a large number of fully sexual individuals, males and females. At swarming time there is little difference in size and shape between the sexes. Both sexes possess long and narrow wings and for a brief period they flutter rather feebly in the sunlight. The swarming flight lasts only for a few minutes but generally it is essential for the life cycle but exceptionally it can be by-passed.

The winged sexuals then pair and drop to the ground. The female (or 'queen') then selects a situation according to species for the founding of a new colony, accompanied by the male. In the Drywood termites the pair fly to a building perhaps by way of the roof-void where, after dropping her wings she lays eggs in a crack in the woodwork. On the other hand the subterranean type female seeks a crack in the earth. When the wings are shed only short stumps are left so that the wings are no impediment to entering narrow spaces. The female rapidly becomes nothing more than an egg-laying machine in a chamber where she is attended by the male. In some species of subterranean termites several eggs are produced every minute for many years. Estimates have been made for the age of a 'queen' in one species as up to 15 years. Two million individuals have been counted in a single nest at one time. Supplementary females can, however, be produced by a number of termite species.

Workers

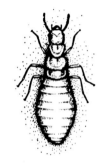

The young termites hatching from the eggs, are either male or female, but they mainly develop into the worker caste in which the sexual organs are rudimentary. The workers which are often of several distinct sizes when fully grown, carry out many different tasks in the community. One of their principal tasks is to forage for food and bring it into the nest, usually in the gut. In a number of species they construct fungus gardens. They feed and look after the termites as well as the queen and king. They excavate the tunnels and build the termitarium – the large mound of earth mixed with saliva which accumulates over the underground part of the living quarters of the nest. They keep the tunnels clean and at the optimum temperature and humidity and they act as the hygiene squad by eating dead individuals.

In almost all species worker termites never venture into the light, spending their whole lives in the dark. If it is necessary to travel away from the nest in search of food then a tunnel of soil particles and saliva is constructed. These mud tubes are a conspicuous feature of the tropical environment and allow subterranean termites to bridge gaps from the ground into buildings and thus may gain entrance to woodwork and books!

Soldiers

Soldier Termite

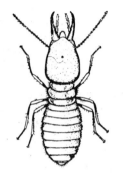

Others of the young hatching termites develop into 'soldiers'. Their function is defence. They guard the nest and attack all marauders such as true ants. The head is large and horny and the mandibles are large and efficient. Sometimes the mandibles are of extraordinary length. The soldier termites are very belligerent and will bite a human finger placed too near. As in the worker caste soldiers are sometimes of two or more sizes. In the soldier caste the shape of the head and size and complexity of the mandibles is often characteristic of species so that in identifying termites the soldier caste must be collected as it will often be that the species can most easily be identified from that caste.

Nasutes

Nasute

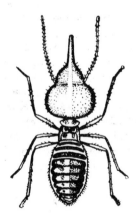

In some termite species a special caste occurs known as the 'nasute'. These have large horny heads but the front is drawn out into a long nose or rostrum from a terminal pore of which a fine stream of toxic or sticky material may be ejected at an enemy. To human beings its aromatic smell is not unpleasant but the sticky mess on the hands is disagreeable.

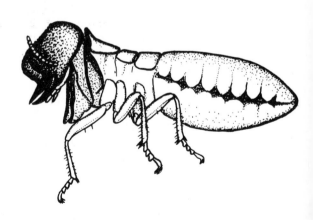

Dry-wood Termite. Soldier Cryptotermes brevis. *Note head fashioned for plugging holes in outer skin of wood or book in emergency. Length 4.5mm.*

HOW TERMITES ARE CLASSIFIED

Main features of the Families

Termites are classified into six families (termite family names end in – TERMITIDAE except TERMOPSIDAE). The first of which, MASTOTERMITIDAE, contains only one species *Mastotermes darwiniensis* which occurs in the Northern Territory of Australia, but is of importance as showing the relationship between termites and cockroaches. In the latter and this single termite species eggs are laid in pods, and there is an anal lobe in the hind-wings.

The second family, the KALOTERMITIDAE, is of great importance on account of the special biological features which gives them the popular name of Dry-wood termites. They are of great economic importance and are important as damaging books wherever they occur which is usually in maritime areas in tropical regions. The worker caste is absent, the work of the community being performed by immature individuals. There is no connection with the ground nor with sources of moisture. Access to the exterior of the woodwork (or books!) is by means of a relatively small hole which can be plugged by the heads of the rudimentary soldier caste. Tunnels may be made using chewed-up wood and saliva to which is added plastic material and other extraneous matter. Soil is not used. The most important identification feature however is the faecal pellets. These are hard and seed-like (sometimes called Poppy-seeds). The pellets are pushed out of the specially made holes mentioned above and accumulate in small piles which are easily identified.

The third family the HODOTERMITIDAE are known as the Harvester termites. They are of negligible importance in buildings. The TERMOPSIDAE, are usually referred to as the Damp-wood termites. The colonies are small and the worker caste is absent as all workers may eventually mature and be capable of reproducing. The RHINOTERMITIDAE are the well-known Subterranean termites. A defensive organ emitting a sticky fluid is present at the front of the head of some of the soldiers. A number of genera are of economic importance including *Heterotermes* and *Reticulitermes*.

The last family, the TERMITIDAE contains about four fifths of all termite species. The soldier caste shows many diverse forms. The mandibles often assume strange and exaggerated shapes. Some of the largest termites known occur in one of the sub-families (MACROTERMITINAE) and in the NASU-TITERMITINAE the soldiers have pear-shaped heads with the 'sticky' gland opening at the tip of the prolongation.

The classification of Termites with coloured illustrations of the main features is shown in an insect poster in Hickin 1971.

IDENTIFICATION OF TERMITE DAMAGE

Although identification of termite species is usually a task for the expert, it should be possible for the book conservator to distinguish damage due to termites from that due to other insect pests and dry-wood termite damage from subterranean.

DRYWOOD TERMITES

The colonies may be very small and occupy only a small volume and indeed theoretically they may occupy only one book. Of the 1,800 described termite species, 80 can be considered as potentially serious pests and of these 14 are members of the family KALOTERMITIDAE – the Dry-wood termites.

Because of the small colony size identification of an attack is difficult in the early stages but later the presence of dry-wood termites can be shown by the occurrence of quantities of the hard faecal pellets often called poppy seed from its similarity. Damage to books is often extensive. Small galleries about 1.5mm can be seen as well as larger about 2.5-3.0mm. Larger flat chambers occur and the faecal pellets are often walled up in sections of the latter. Shelter tubes are not normally present and the galleries are not stained with earth brought out by the termites.

SUBTERRANEAN TERMITES

The colonies may be very large and shelter tubes of the colour of the local earth, are usually conspicuous often bridging brickwork from the ground to the interior of the building. Breaking the shelter tube will usually reveal abundant termites passing backwards and forwards. Book damage by subterranean termites is shown by frequent staining, absent of faecal pellets and great diversity in size and shape of tunnels and chambers.

TERMITE SPECIES INJURIOUS TO BOOKS

It would be difficult to over-estimate the potential threat to books in those tropical and subtropical areas of the world where termites occur. Bansa (1981) wrote that 'In tropical and sub-tropical climates there is the threat of damage by insects of a nature and to an extent that is unknown in moderate climate zones'. There are several reasons for this. Termites occur in extremely large numbers yet often serious damage can occur before any obvious signs of injury are observed. Without constant vigilance damage to books can proceed to utter destruction – a situation which seldom occurs with other insect pests.

In recent years however with a greater knowledge of the biology of termites, destruction on such a scale does not take place so often but the potential hazard to books remains. Also the situation has improved to a great extent with the establishment of pest control firms on a wide scale. In many countries these companies work to agreed procedures and comply with safety regulations.

CHAPTER FIVE

PSOCOPTERA
Psocids, Booklice

This insect order is known also as CORRODENTIA and COPEOGNATHA. The species of this order are all small in size and are often minute. Some are less than one mm in length and no species is known of a greater length than 10mm. About 1,700 species have been described and they are found throughout the world except for the circum-polar regions!

To the naked eyes a psocid is recognised, apart from its small size, by its comparatively large mobile head, emphasised by the conspicuous neck-like area. The eyes are usually large, dark in colour and convex. Seen from the side the insect appears hump-backed. The antennae are long and threadlike and consist of some 13 to 20 segments, usually the former. The mouthparts of psocids are characterised by possessing a strong rod-like organ furnished with three teeth at one end. This is called the 'maxillary pick'.

The first thoracic segment (prothorax) is usually very small and the terminal leg segment (tarsus) is 2- or 3-segmented. Cerci (rod-like protuberances arising from the end of the abdomen) are not present. Rather delicate membraneous wings are sometimes present and are held tent-wise over the body.

A number of species are associated with Man's domestic environment including some which cause injury to books but most are found on or under the barks of trees, in birds' nests or amongst vegetation especialy where algae, lichens and fungi occur. A number of species feed on moulds (species of fungi) and often carry their spores entangled amongst their bodyhairs. Many psocid species live gregariously under loose tree-bark protected by a silken web and appear to be loose family groups. Swarms of certain psocid species are known to occur in buildings.

Psocids are said usually not to be harmful to man and are generally included in the category of nuisance. Actually they are more than this in that they are important as a signal that conditions conducive to more important injurious insect infestations are present. Humidity must be lowered, rate of air change increased and fungal hyphae removed.

On the other hand, however, when conditions have been suitable for the large scale reproduction of these insects in buildings – warm humid atmosphere and little disturbance – great anxiety has been caused to householders and, particularly in the United States, there are many records of costly lawsuits due to complaints that premises were unsuitable for human habitation and pest control companies have often been involved.

Several aspects of the biology of psocids are of special interest. Firstly, egg-size. The eggs of psocids (at least in those species which have been studied) are of relatively enormous size, that of *Liposcelis* being about one-third of the length of the female.

Secondly, the phenomenon of noise production; this is produced by the species *Trogium pulsatorium* which was known to Linnaeus and for two centuries there was confusion as to which insect was causing the tapping noises in the 'stilly watches of the night'. Was it the beetle now known as the Death Watch beetle, *Xestobium rufovillosum* or a psocid? We quote the letter from the Reverend Mr William Derham of Upminster, July 21, 1701 'The Insect which makes this long Beating, is a small greyish Insect, much resembling a louse, when looked on only with the naked Eye. For which reason (for want of another name) I call it *Pediculus Pulsatorius*. It is very nimble in running to seek its shelter, when disturbed. It is very common in all parts of the House, in the Summer months'.

In fact both insects tap. In *Trogium pulsatorium* the noise is made by the abdomen striking the surface on which it is standing. It is best heard when the insect is on paper. Other species are known to tap but in some, such as *Liposcelis* spp.,

55

it is unknown. It is of interest to note that in the closely related termites (ISOPTERA) some species will suddenly halt in their activities and vibrate the abdomen for no apparent reason.

Thirdly, in some species there is a suppression of the male sex. Throughout a long series of experiments with *Liposcelis granicola* no male was produced but unfertilised eggs developed normally. This phenomenon is known as parthenogenesis.

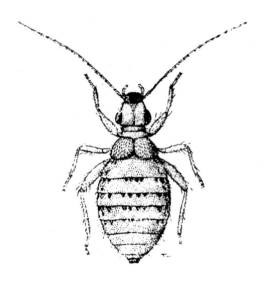

Book Louse Trogium pulsatorium. *Whitish in colour with dark marks. About 1.5mm in length.*

BOOK LOUSE

Latin: *Trogium pulsatorium*
American: *Death watch*
French: *Psoque*

Description of Adult Stage

About 1.5mm in length. Whitish in colour, whole body covered with fine hairs. Abdomen broadly oval with a series of small dark marks at the front margin of the abdominal segments 2 to 4, and fainly on 5.

Distribution

Almost cosmopolitan. Occurs as one of commonest psocid species in warehouses and ships' holds.

Time of Emergence

Under household conditions this species is fully grown by August/September.

Feeding Habits

Probably only feeds on fungal hyphae but in doing so damages the material on which the fungus is growing.

Type of Damage to Books

Glue and paste used in bookbinding are recorded as being eaten but these materials were most probably damp and supporting mould growth, and it is most probably the latter on which psocids feed.

Length of Life Cycle

Generally an annual life cycle under usual household conditions.

BOOK LOUSE

Latin: *Liposcelis bostrychophilus* Badonnel. This is the species widely recorded as *Liposcelis divinatorious* (Mueller) and as *Liposcelis granicola* (Broadhead and Hobby)

American: *Book Louse*
French: *Pou des livres*
German: *Bucherlause*
Spanish: *Piojos de los libros*

A detailed experimental study of this species (as *L. granicola*) was carried out by Broadhead and Hobby in 1944.

Description of Adult Stage

About 1.0mm in length, semi-transparent body, dull brown with reddish-brown head; older individuals have yellowish-brown irregular patches on head. Antennae are 15-segmented. Seven eye facets in each eye. Abdomen sparsely covered with very short hairs, longer bristles at rear end of abdomen. Wing pads absent.

Distribution

Occurs as a pest in stored food products in Britain and probably introduced widespread. It is probably commonest species found in dwellings and libraries.

Time of Emergence

It is probable that active nymphs may occur whenever satisfactory conditions arise.

Feeding Habits

In the laboratory, cultures were maintained on yeast and wholemeal flour with various additives including mould.

Type of Damage to Books

Glues and pastes are recorded as being eaten.

Length of Life Cycle

The average duration of nymphal stage under laboratory conditions was from 15 to 31 days at 25°C and 75-76 per cent Relative Humidity. It is long-lived as an adult. Under the same conditions the average length of adult life varied from 175 to 268 days according to type of food-stuff.

Immature Stages

EGG. About 0.3mm – one third of the body-length of the female, smooth and bluish-white in colour. Incubation period is 11 days at 25°C and 75 per cent Relative Humidity. At first 3 eggs are laid daily and about 200 eggs were laid in six months. The egg stage lasts on average eleven days.

NYMPH. Hatches from the egg by means of a saw-like 'egg-burster'. It resembles the adult except it is more fragile in appearance and paler in colour. It undergoes four nymphal stages before assuming the adult stage. No wings are developed at any stage. The nymphal period is only about 15 days at 25°C and 75 per cent Relative Humidity.

Other species commonly found in buildings are:

Nymphopsocus destructor. Whitish in colour. Rather like *Trogium pulsatorium* but devoid of black spots on the abdomen.

Lepinotus inquilinus. Very dark and often blackish when mature. Wing pads present.

Lepinotus patruelis. Very dark and often blackish when mature. Wing pads present.

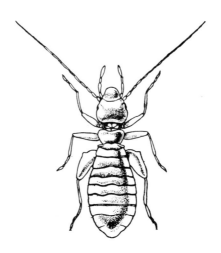

Book Louse Liposcelis bostrychophilus.
Semi-transparent dull-brown body. About 1.0mm in length.

59

CHAPTER SIX
LEPIDOPTERA
Moths

Moths, together with butterflies constitute the order LEPIDOPTERA. The name of this order literally means 'scaly-winged' and indeed the large showy wings are covered with minute scales arranged on the wings like the tiles of a house and are characteristically bright in colour and patterned in intricate designs. This makes the LEPIDOPTERA the most easily recognizable of all insects. The head bears a pair of antennae which are long and segmented and occur in a number of forms. In butterflies the antennae terminate in knobs. In some moths they are comb-like and in some others they resemble feathers but are generally thread-like. The compound eyes are conspicuous and hemispherical. Mandibles are absent except in the most primitive families but the mouthparts (the maxillae) are modified to form a long tube-like proboscis. This is tightly coiled under the head when not in use but when sucking liquids such as nectar it is extended and in some species it is of extraordinary length. The two pairs of wings exhibit an intricate venation pattern often of importance in identification.

There is complete metamorphosis during the life-cycle, the egg stage is followed by an active larval stage during which growth takes place, this is followed by an immobile pupal stage and finally the adult insect emerges.

About 100,000 species have been described. In size, moths vary enormously from minute to as much as 250mm across the outstretched wings and the bodies are often as large as or even larger than a small mammal.

The number of species of LEPIDOPTERA recorded from buildings where they are injurious to man's economy however is less than forty. The number of species of importance to the book conservator is only five and all belong to a small group of families (superfamily) known as the TINEINA. Not all the five species are recorded as damaging books but all are likely to have done so in the past and may on occasions do so again unless special book storage precautions, which are described later, are undertaken.

A number of other species are of great importance as injuring a number of stored food products such as grain, flour, dried fruit and other foodstuffs, as well as tobacco. All belong to the group of families (superfamily) PYRALIDINA. None of the latter however are recorded as damaging books and it is unlikely that they would do so.

The TINEINA includes two families of which the TINEIDAE, known as the Clothes moths and the OECOPHORIDAE known as the House moths, are involved. These two families are easily identified by the manner in which the wings are held when at rest. The TINEIDAE includes the three species known as Clothes moths:

> *Tineola bisselliella* Hummel (Common Clothes moth)
> *Tinea pellionella* L. (Case-bearing Clothes moth)

and *Trichopaga tapetzella* L. (White-tip Clothes moth or Tapestry moth)

In these species the wings are held tent-wise at an acute angle over the abdomen when the insect is at rest.

In the family OECOPHORIDAE the two species are known as House moths:

> *Hofmannophila pseudospretella* Staint. (Brown House moth)

and *Endrosis sarcitrella* Steph. (White-shouldered House moth).

In these species the wings are held more or less flat over the abdomen, scissor-wise when the insect is at rest.

61

COMMON CLOTHES MOTH

Latin: *Tineola biselliella* Hum.
American: *Webbing Clothes Moth*
French: *Teigne des vetements, Teigne de la laine*
German: *Kleidermotte*
Spanish: *Polilla común de las pieles*

Description of Adult Stage

Length from head to tips of folded wings is from 6 to 8mm and wing span is from 10 to 15mm. This large size variation depends on food suitability (see later). The wings and body are 'shining golden' and distinguished from the following species, *Tinaea pellionella*, by the absence of any spots or marking whatsoever. The apex and outer margin of the forewings and almost all the margin of the hindwings are fringed by very long hairs which give a false impression of wing size. The antennae are long and threadlike, the eyes black and the head is covered by long scale-like hairs which give a helmet-like appearance. The legs similarly are furnished with long bristle-like scales which give a spikey fringe to them. There is no trace of a coiled proboscis as is found in most moths.

Distribution

Europe, America and Australia, and probably cosmopolitan.

Time of Emergence

In heated buildings adults emerge at any time of the year but otherwise are on the wing from May to July.

Feeding Habits

A long list of materials have been recorded as being eaten by the larvae of the Common Clothes moth. Included are furs, imperfectly cleaned animal skeletons, mammal and bird skins, insect specimens, mummified cadavers, material in bird nests and the cells of wild bees, beefmeal, fishmeal, pemmican casein, milk products and fingernail clippings. In experimental work the larvae thrived on bristles, hairs, feathers, fur and raw wool and did not do so well on woollen cloth.

62

Indeed, they were not able to complete their development on clean woollen fabrics. In the home they are most often found infesting woollen garments that have been soiled with perspiration, urine or spilt food (soup etc.).

Type of Damage to Books

Woollen cloth binding and also silk is eaten out in irregular patches and covered with a webbing produced from the spinnerets beneath the mouth of the larva. Silken tunnels mixed with faecal pellets are also formed in which the larva rests. A characteristic of moth damage to books is the presence of tough oval cocoons about 10mm in length in which pupation takes place. The empty pupal skin often protrudes from the cocoon after emergence. The binding and paper is often bitten out when the cocoon is being spun. Note that exit holes are not present.

Immature Stages

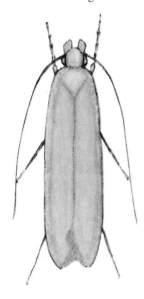

Common Clothes Moth
Tineola biselliella

EGG. The oval egg is ivory-white 0.5 x 0.3mm in size and minutely reticulated. When laid they are covered with a gelatinous film with which the egg adheres to the woollen fibres but does not prevent it from being shaken out. The female usually commences laying about 24 hours after emergence. The average number of eggs laid is between 40 and 50 although 221 have been recorded from one female. At 15°C the egg hatches in 24 days and at 25°C seven days.

LARVA. The newly-hatched larva is 1.0mm in length and but only 0.2mm in width and is creamy-white except for the head which is golden brown. The fully-fed larva is about 10mm in length and the colour of the head becomes rather darker. The three segments of the thorax each bears a pair of segmented legs terminating with a sharp claw. In addition abdominal segments 3 to 6 inclusive each bear a pair of large sucker-like pro-legs each furnished with a circlet of minute hooks and the abdomen terminates with a pair of larger pro-legs known as the anal claspers.

The larva usually spins a tube of silk open at each end in which it rests. Incorporated in the tube are pieces of bitten-off fibre and faecal pellets. Sometimes instead of a tube a web shelters the larva as it crawls about. In addition the larva constructs a cylindrical case in which it moults or rests for longer periods. This can be easily differentiated from the portable larval case of the following species, *Tinaea pellionella,* which is altogether neater and tidier.

Progression however, is usually made by first spinning a carpet of silk on which the larva walks along. A silken oval cocoon is constructed in which pupation takes place.

PUPA. Varies from 4 to 7mm in length and is torpedo-shaped, blunt at the anterior end but tapering to the anal end. The tips of the appendages are free and thus differs from the pupa of most moths. About four of the abdominal segments are capable of wriggling and there are six rows of minute hooks on the abdomen which enable the pupa to emerge from the cocoon before the back splits to release the moth. Like other members of the LEPIDOPTERA the wings are small and flaccid at first but expand by the pumping of fluid through the veins in the wings. Within half to one hour the wings attain their final size, they dry and the moth is ready for flight.

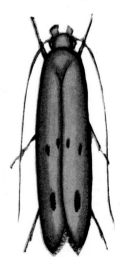

Case-bearing Clothes Moth
Tinea pellionella

THE CASE-BEARING CLOTHES MOTH

Latin: *Tinea pellionella*
American: *Casemaking Clothes Moth*
French: *Teigne des fourrures, Mite des vetements*
German: *Pelzmotte*
Spanish: *Polilla portaestuches de los roperos*

Description of Adult Stage

This is similar in general appearance to the Common Clothes Moth but is rather smaller. The wing colour however is slightly darker and there are three indistinct dark marks present on the forewings. Their size and distinctness is somewhat variable.

Distribution

Abundant in Europe, common in North America although not nearly so common as the Common Clothes moth. Introduced into Australia and is probably found world-wide.

Time of Emergence

In heated buildings adults emerge at any time of year but otherwise are on the wing from May to July.

Feeding Habits

Feathers, wool and animal hairs and bristles are the usual materials on which it feeds so that garments, furs and piano-felts are most usually infested. In addition however, the larvae are known to feed on a wide variety of drugs more or less poisonous to human beings.

Type of Damage to Books

This is similar to that caused by the Common Clothes Moth, irregular patches bitten out of woollen cloth and browsing of longer wool fibres. In addition the pupal case may damage any part of a book except in the leaves. No webbing silk is present but the larvae in their cases are sometimes difficult to detect.

Length of Life Cycle

In the northern United States there is one generation a year with the moths in evidence from June to August, but in the southern states there are two generations annually and in centrally heated dwellings eggs are laid throughout the year.

Immature Stages

EGG. Whereas the egg of the Common Clothes Moth has a minute reticulated pattern, that of the Case-bearing Clothes Moth is longitudinally ridged.

LARVA. The larva is easily identified by the case which it constructs and which it drags about with it wherever it walks. The hinder end of the body is always hidden within the case and the whole larva disappears within it if menaced. The case is elongated, open at both ends, slightly flattened and widest at the middle, but it enlarges at front and rear ends. The inside of the case is smooth but the outside is rough and faecal pellets and pieces of bitten off fibres adhere. Because the outside of the case resembles the material on which the larva is feeding it is often camouflaged so well that it makes detection difficult. The larva never abandons its case. The case is enlarged by the larva making a longitudinal cut then inserting a V-shaped patch.

PUPA. Prior to pupation both ends of the case are sealed and the change to pupa takes place within.

WHITE-TIP CLOTHES MOTH or TAPESTRY MOTH

Latin:	*Trichophaga tapetzella*
American:	*Tapestry* or *Carpet Moth*
French:	*Mites des tapis, Mite* or *teigne des tapisseries*
German:	*Tapetenmotte*
Spanish:	*Polilla blanca y negra de las tapicerias*

Description of Adult Stage

This is the largest of the three species of clothes moth. The wing span is from 22 to 25mm and the length from head to apex of wings is from 8 to 10mm. The female is usually the larger. It is easy to identify by its white head and the basal one-third of the forewings is black whilst the remainder is white speckled with black and grey. The shape of the wings is similar to the other two clothes moth species. The moth resembles a bird dropping.

Distribution

Europe, rare in the United States.

Time of Emergence

The adults are found from April to June and there may be a second emergence in August to October.

Feeding Habits

Recorded as infesting woollen materials such as blankets, horsehair stuffing in harness, tapestries and carpets. It is also a notable pest of fur and feathers. It would appear that this insect was more important as a pest especially of books, in the past, when book storage conditions in respect of humidity, temperature and hygiene were favourable to the insect. The larva constructs a silken tube which tunnels into the material on (or in) which it is feeding.

Type of Damage to Books

This has not been specifically recorded.

Length of Life Cycle

One and in favourable circumstances two generations annually.

Immature Stages

EGG. From 60 to 100 eggs are laid in batches from April to June and sometimes from August to October.

LARVA. Four to six moults take place during larval life. A pupal case (cocoon) is formed.

PUPA. The pupa partially wriggles out of the cocoon before the adult emerges.

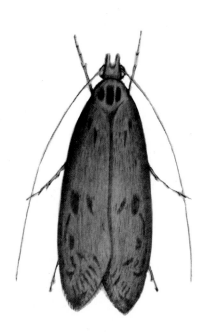

Brown House Moth
Hofmannophila pseudospretella

BROWN HOUSE MOTH

Latin: *Hofmannophila* (formerly referred to the genus *Borkhausenia*) *pseudospretella* (Staint.)
American: *Brown House Moth*
French: *Mite brune*
German: *Samenmotte*
Spanish: *Polilla domestica parda*

Description of Adult Stage

The head, thorax and forewings brown, the general background colour varying from dark olive-brown to a light buff. The thorax and forewings are speckled with dark flecks in a variable manner but on each forewing there are several large spots. Across the expanded wings the male measures from 17 to 19mm whilst the female measures from about 18 to over 25mm. When at rest the male measures from head to wingtip about 8.5mm whilst the female measures about 14.5mm in length. When disturbed, it runs quickly to hide in dark folds or crevices, and in fact like the preceding species, those actually flying are most likely to be males or spent females.

Distribution

Abundant in Europe, more common in England than elsewhere, occasionally damages woollens and other fabrics in the United States, introduced into Australia and is probably practically cosmopolitan.

Time of Emergence

In England the moth flies from May to October.

Feeding Habits

The larvae are known to feed on a wide variety of materials in dwellings, warehouses and other types of premises in Britain. It is probably of greatest importance as a pest of stored food products including cereals and cereal products, but it is well known as a general feeder infesting woollen clothing and blankets, and such diverse materials as wine corks, birds nests and chicken meal as well as various foodstuffs left overlong in tins in the pantry. It is of some importance as a pest of leather bookbinding.

69

Type of Damage to Books	The larva forms a furrow or channel wherever there is a crease such as between the back and the front covers. Here it browses on the surface of the leather within a few strands of silk and a few faecal pellets.
Length of Life Cycle	There is thought to be one generation a year but in premises heated during the winter there may be two.
Immature Stages	EGG. The eggs are laid singly, usually on rough surfaces and are hard and shiny, not sticky, 0.5-0.6mm in length.

LARVA reaching a length of 18 to 20mm this shining white and rather naked looking larva has a chestnut-coloured head as well as a plate on the first thoracic segment. It spins very little silk except when feeding on loose, friable materials such as chicken meal or farinaceous meals of various sorts. The wide range of materials which it will infest has been mostly covered as above but mention must be made of its ability to subsist on wool fluff and bread crumbs in the gaps between floorboards. The latter may be bare or covered by carpets, linoleum or plastic floor covering. The phenomenon of *diapause* is exhibited by this species and book conservators should have some knowledge of it. This is the ability of the larva to tide over a period of unfavourable conditions by assuming a resting, non-active condition. It spins a thin but tough cocoon and lives upon its reserve food material. This may occur during very cold weather but it often takes place for unaccountable reasons. It is thought that sometimes an inherited rhythmic periodicity may provoke diapause. At the end of the diapause, the larva bites its way out of the cocoon and recommences feeding.

PUPA. A tough silken torpedo-shaped cocoon is constructed by the larva, usually in a fold of the infested material. The length of the pupal stage is given as about ten days.

WHITE SHOULDERED HOUSE MOTH

Latin: *Endrosis sarcitrella* Steph. (sometimes referred to as *lactella*)

Description of Adult Stage
The head and the front of the thorax is white giving a cape-like effect. The forewings are greyish or greyish-brown, mottled with darker and lighter tones. The length from head to tip of wings, in the resting position, in the male is 6mm whilst the female may be much larger at 10.5mm. Across the wings from wing-tip to wing-tip the male measures up to about 14.5mm, whilst he female measures from 17mm to about 22mm. This is the species often encountered by the housewife when it has dropped into a jug of milk or water left overnight, and its struggles on the surface are evident by the trail of scales which are left. (The attraction of the milk jug obviously inspired the specific name *lactella* which was used at one time).

Distribution
Widely distributed and commonly found throughout the British Isles. It never assumes however, the importance as a pest as the preceding species. It ocurs throughout the world.

Time of Emergence
The adult stage occurs from May to October.

Feeding Habits
The larvae damage much the same range of materials as do those of the Brown House moth, but probably materials of vegetable origin are attacked to a greater extent. Peas, seed potatoes and other seeds, rubbish in bird nests, old roof thatch, fungi on trees and all kinds of vegetable refuse. It must be borne in mind however that old vegetable refuse usually contains dead insects and spiders, mouse and bird droppings or otherwise contaminated with animal matter. When this and the preceding species are found infesting the same material the Brown House moth predominates.

71

Type of Damage to Books	Not specifically reported.
Length of Life Cycle	Almost certainly an annual life cycle.
Immature Stages	EGG. The eggs are dull white and sticky and they adhere together, about 0.55mm in length. LARVA. Grows to about 13mm in length and is ivory white in colour with a brown head. They are to be found throughout the year. PUPA. Similar to the preceding species.

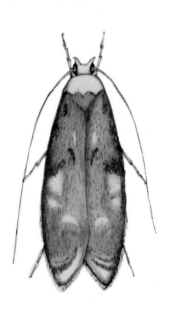

White Shouldered House Moth
Endrosis sarcitrella

CHAPTER SEVEN

COLEOPTERA

Beetles
Dermestid beetles

The Order COLEOPTERA is the most highly developed insect group – all species are known as beetles. There are about a quarter of a million different species and thus outnumber all other insect groups. Beetle biology is most diverse and no other insect group has invaded land, water and the air to anything like the same extent. Except for living animals almost every form of organic matter is utilized as food. It comes as no surprise therefore to learn that a number of beetle species are pests of books especially old books.

A beetle in the adult stage is usually fairly easily recognized even by the layman. The most characteristic feature is the horny wing-cases known as the elytra which usually cover the second and third segments of the thorax and the abdomen as well as the folded-up wings which arise from the third thoracic segment. The elytra are indeed the highly modified first pair of wings which arise from the second thoracic segment.

Three families of beetles are represented amongst those insects which damage books DERMESTIDAE, ANOBIIDAE and PTINIDAE. The book-damaging species in the DERMESTIDAE are dealt with in this chapter whilst those in the ANOBIIDAE are described in Chapter 8 and those in the PTINIDAE in Chapter 9.

The DERMESTIDAE consists of small or moderately small beetles with the body clothed with scales or fine hair sometimes giving a characteristic pattern. They are usually referred to as the hide and carpet beetles. About 700 species are known worldwide of which 17 occur in Britain. A number of them occur as cosmopolitan pests and are of commercial importance. As the name signifies many are known as 'skin' eaters, the larvae feeding on skins, hides, fur and wool but in addition occur in a wide range of dry material of animal origin which is rich in protein. Examples are dried and smoked fish, dead insects in museum cabinets as well as around spiders' webs, smoked meat, silkworm pupae and eggs, animal skins and feathers in museums, dried carcases (dermestid larvae have been used to clean skeleton specimens in museums) and the nests of birds and rodents. When the latter are situated in and around buildings it is thought that dermestid infestations originate from such situations. This is of great importance when considering library hygiene.

It is however as pests of leather that makes dermestid beetles of the greatest importance to those responsible for the safe-keeping of leather-bound books.

There are about 50 known species of the genus *Dermestes* but only three species are well-known as pests.

BACON BEETLE

Latin: *Dermestes lardarius*
American: *Larder beetle*
French: *Dermeste du lard*
German: *Gemeiner Speckkafer*
Spanish: *Escarabajo de las despensas*

Description of Adult Stage

From 7 to 9mm in length and elongate oval in shape, the prothorax almost as wide as the elytra. The anterior half of the elytra pale yellowish which is traversed by a black band usually broken up into three spots. The rest of the body dark brown. The undersurface as well as the legs, covered with fine yellow hairs. The male can be identified by the round shiny area with a tuft of red bristles at the centre of the third and fourth abdominal segment on the ventral surface.

Distribution

A pest in Europe generally, as well as the United States and Canada and Australia and may well be cosmopolitan.

Time of Emergence

Spring and Summer.

Feeding habits

Adult beetles feed on similar substances to those of the larvae. Ham, bacon, dried and smoked meats, cheese, museum specimens, stored tobacco, dog biscuits, dead insects as well as young birds (chicken, ducklings and pigeons).

Type of Book Damage

The contribution to insect book damage by *Dermestes lardarius* was studied extensively by O. V. Kozulina in the Department for the Care and Preservation of Books in the Lenin Library, Moscow, 1953 and it is from her account that the notes which follow are taken. The larvae first attack the inner side of the leather, making pits, boreholes or perforations. If the inner side of the leather cover is protected on all sides by paper or cardboard, the larvae and the adult beetles will attack the shiny upper face of the cover. The face of the leather then becomes covered with rough 'bald spots'. The beetles will dig holes and perforate the cover, which disintegrates as a result.

75

The larvae when fully-fed, bore large holes into books in order to construct a pupation chamber. This may occur at the edges inside the body of the book or from the base. 'Broadcloth' is mentioned as the hairs being eaten first by dermestids whether this specifically involved *D. lardarius* is not clear.

Length of Life Cycle

Estimations of the length of Life cycle are complicated by the fact that the adults may live for over 22 months. Mating begins 'in the first days of Spring'. The adults die quickly when deprived of moisture. Mating takes place between mid-March and May. The mating period lasts up to 4 months. The adults shun light and are active only at night. In some conditions as many as five complete life cycles occur per year although an annual life cycle has also been reported.

EGG. Sausage-shaped and white in colour. About 2mm in length by 0.6mm in width. Laid in parallel rows. When laid in books they are found in the spine and in leaves which have been folded for a long period, or between the outside cover of the book and a close fitting adjacent book. They hatch on about the sixth day (20°C and 70 per cent Relative Humidity).

LARVA. The newly-hatched larva is from 2.5-3.0mm in length with translucent skin and covered with reddish-brown bristles. The fully-fed larvae are from 10-15mm in length and about 3.0mm in width. They are covered with short and long reddish-brown bristles. An important character however is the presence of a pair of spines on the penultimate abdominal segment. They arise nearly at right angles to the body but the tips are directed backwards. A conspicuous median bristle is absent (present in *D. maculatus*). There are usually 5 or 6 moults but as many as 12 have been recorded. The female larvae are believed to have an additional moult compared with larvae destined to be males). If disturbed whilst feeding the larva often 'freezes' in a curled position as though feigning death. It is when seeking a pupation site that extensive damage to books is often caused. The larva will tunnel into almost anything which their jaws are capable of scraping. The borehole thus produced may be anything from just the length of the larva to about 30cm and a number of instances are known when severe loss has been occasioned including the sinking of ships. Increase in temperature from 20° to 24.5°C at approximately the same Relative Humidity 68-69 per cent, increased the period of the complete life cycle from 70.4 days to 93.0 days. Larvae of *Dermestes lardarius* die quite quickly if deprived of food but are quick to cannibalise (and adults too). Eggs of their own species are readily eaten as well as larvae, being particularly vulnerable immediately after moulting when they are immobile. Kozulina carried out a comprehensive series of experiments on damaging effect of *Dermestes lardarius* and other dermestids on books under laboratory conditions. She found that larvae develop into pupae and adult beetles only if able to feed on animal protein. The growth of the larvae is stunted and they die before pupation if they are only able to feed on vegetable materials, old leather or on silk. If the larvae are able to feed on a mixed diet, they feed on *all* the constituents. The larvae and adult beetles will feed on all constituent materials of books although any animal protein is consumed first.

PUPA. Pale yellow in colour at first and the larval cuticle is cast off at pupation unless it is unable to make a burrow in which case pupation takes place within the larval skin. This stage usually lasts from 8 to 14 days but about two days before the adult beetle emerges, the pupa turns brown particularly where the elytra show through the pupal cuticle. The terminal abdominal spines as seen in the larva are retained by the pupa.

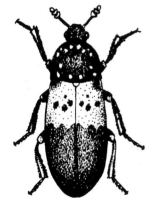

The Bacon Beetle Dermestes lardarius *7-9mm.*

77

THE LEATHER BEETLE

Latin:	*Dermestes maculatus* (De geer) In some accounts this species is referred to as *Dermestes vulpinus* (Fabricius)
American:	*Hide* or *Leather Beetle*
French:	*Dermeste*
German:	*Dornspeckkafer*
Spanish:	*Escarabajo del tocino*

Description of Adult Stage

It varies in size from 5 to 10mm in length. Elytra are completely black in colour although when freshly emerged may be brownish. Shape is similar to *Dermestes lardarius* but the elytra terminate in a fine point. The undersurface is mostly white. They fly readily and known to enter windows near their breeding site.

Distribution

Cosmopolitan. Distributed by world wide commerce in hides and skins.

Time of Emergence

May be found at any time of the year but are usually occur in the greatest numbers during Spring and Summer.

Feeding Habits

Prefers hides and skins and thrives on smoked meat and dried cheese.

Type of Damage to Books

Not specifically recorded but likely to be similar to *D. lardarius* as larvae are known to wander widely and bore into almost any compact substance when seeking a pupation site. Faecal pellets of larva sometimes joined together like row of beads. Important for identification.

Length of Life Cycle

There may be as many as six generations in a year and the adults live for up to three months during which time they feed on similar substances as eaten by the larvae but not so voraciously. At average temperatures and humidity the life cycle takes 60 to 70 days.

Immature Stages

EGG. 2mm in length, creamy white in colour, laid singly or in batches of up to 20 in cracks.

Oviposition ceases if egg laying sites are not available. One female has been recorded as laying 845 eggs. In 2 to 12 days eggs hatch.

LARVA. Extremely hairy and very agile. They undergo the first moult after two days and in favourable circumstances moult about every 5 days thereafter averaging about 7 moults but up to 11 have been recorded. They avoid light. They may be distinguished from larvae of D. *lardarius* by the spines on the penultimate abdominal segment sloping backwards but with the extremities directed forwards and there is a conspicuous median bristle arising slightly behind them. Length of larva when fully grown between 10 and 15mm.

PUPA. The pronotum is covered with short bristles and bristles are present on the abdominal segments. The terminal abdominal spines present on the larvae and also present on the pupae. The length of the pupal stage is about 7 days.

Two species of the dermestid genus *Attagenus* are important pests in buildings in many parts of the world due to the larvae feeding on woollen materials. The adults are intermediate in size between those of *Dermestes* and *Anthrenus*.

Leather Beetle or Hide Beetle Dermestes maculatus. *From 5 to 10mm in length. Wing cases black and terminating in fine point.*

BLACK CARPET BEETLE

Latin:	*Attagenus unicolor* Brahm

American: *Black Carpet beetle*
French: *Attagène*
German: *Dunkler Peltzkafer*
Spanish: *Escarabajo negro de las tapicerias*

Description of Adult Stage

The size varies between 2.8 to 5.0mm in length and in colour it is uniformly black or very dark brown with yellowish-red legs, and ventral surface covered with thick yellow hair. The contour of the body is elongate oval and the antennae are clubbed. Males can be differentiated from females by the terminal segment of the antennae of the male being twice as long as those of the female.

Time of Emergence

Adults of this species occur from the end of April to August. They seek certain flowers out of doors when freshly emerged (*Spiraea* is specially mentioned both in Europe and North America) and also the flowers of UMBELLIFERAE, and here they feed on pollen and nectar and mate.

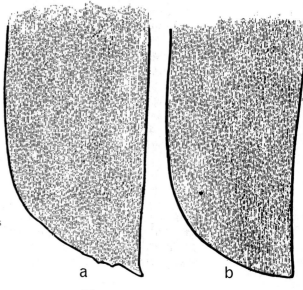

7.3
Apex of wing cases of
(a) Leather Beetle Dermestes maculatus
(b) Other species of Dermestes.

a   b

Type of Damage to Books	Kozulina reports that damage is caused to leather, cloth and silk bindings of books. The upper face of the leather corners of the binding eaten and the surface pitted. The excreta is variously coloured according to the part of the book being consumed. When feeding on paper the excreta is snow-white, but black in the case of print and light brown in the case of glue and leather. Although the larvae will feed on old leather binding for some months they are not able to complete their development and die out but in the case of freshly-tanned leather (which has a much higher fat content) development is completed. The larvae thrive on broadcloth and will live for up to five months on paper alone.
Feeding Habits	Back and Cotton 1938 record a long list of materials known to have been infested by the larvae of this species. Woollen rugs, clothing, silk, carpeting, felts, furs, skins, yarn, velvet, feathers, hair-filled mattresses and upholstered furniture, wool-filled blankets, house insulations containing sheep wool and cattle hair, meat and insect meal, kid leather, milk powders, casein, books, birds' nests, cayenne peppers and many seeds and grains. It is also known to damage raw silk in Japan. The larvae are able to bore into food containers of various substances and thus give entry to their contents to other pest species that would otherwise be kept out. The larvae are repelled by light and roll up and feign death if disturbed. The adults require to drink free water before eggs are laid and when feeding.
Length of the Life Cycle	Much depends on the diet of the larvae. At average room temperature and humidity Kozulina found that larvae moulted 12 times and had a 2-year life cycle (foodstuff not specified) but with a mixed diet supplemented by freshly dried cricket (presumably *Gryllulus domesticus*), and at average temperature of 20.8°C and 69 per cent Relative Humidity, an intensive growth rate was

81

exhibited and the life cycle was completed in one year after 8 larval moults.

Immature Stages

EGG. The small pearly-white eggs are laid on the 7th day after mating if free moisture is available. They are laid on broadcloth or on the inner side of Morocco leather under library conditions and are attached to the hairs of the wool and fibres of leather or to 'fluff' in cracks. They are laid in small heaps or scattered. 60 eggs were found to be average per female but in one case 139 was noted. The egg membrane is very thin and is easily injured. They hatch after 12-15 days.

LARVA. Long, cylindrical in shape but tapering towards the hinder end. At first straw-coloured the larvae darken at each succeeding stage, and depending on the nature of the food becoming reddish-golden-brown. The tergal plates appear which give conspicuous banded appearance to the larva and to the moulted skins which are a characteristic feature of an *Attagenus* infestation.

When fully-grown the larva measures about 7-8mm in length and has a strange way of walking appearing to glide rather like a millipede. The length of the larval life under normal room temperature varies from 258 to 639 days approximating to a one or two year life cycle but there is a wide variation in the number of moults from five to as many as twenty under adverse conditions.

PUPA. Pupation takes place within the last larval skin and may last from 6 to 24 days. It takes place in the Spring and early Summer, April to June and the adult remains within the larval/pupal skin for some days before emerging from 2 to 20 days have been recorded.

Adult length
of Life

Both sexes live for a little over a month.

THE CARPET BEETLE

Latin:	*Attagenus pellio* (L.)
American:	*Black Carpet beetle*
French:	*Attagene, attagene des pelleteries, attagene des fourrures*
German:	*Pelzkafer*
Spanish:	*Escarabajo de las pieles*

Description of Adult Stage

Attagenus pellio resembles *A. unicolor* in size and shape but differs in the possession of a white or yellowish spot in the centre of each elytron. This is a most conspicuous feature and of great importance in aiding identification. The whole body is covered by brownish black hair. The length of the male measures from 3.6 to 5.7mm and the width from 1.8 to 3.0mm.

Distribution

Both above species occur in Europe, Asia, Africa, North America and Australia but whereas *A. pellio* is the most abundant pest in Europe, it is *A. unicolor* that is the serious pest in North America.

Time of Emergence

Most probably the adult emerges in Spring and early Summer as it is found at this time on flowers (Hawthorn, Wild plum and *Spiraea* have been recorded) feeding on nectar. The female is known to live up to 75 days if unmated.

Feeding Habits

The larvae have been found attacking or associated with birds' nests, beehives, furs, woollen materials, dried museum specimens, old bones, smoked meat and fish, dried egg, casein, bolting silk, grain and cereal products, dried plants (in some cases the larvae were feeding on the bodies of other dead infesting insects). Out of doors the larvae are mostly found in birds' nests, those of the House Sparrow and warehouses are often a reservoir of infestation in dwellings.

Type of Damage to Books

Not specified.

| Length of Life Cycle | Usually one generation annually but on occasion may last three years or as little as six months. |

Length of
Life Cycle

Usually one generation annually but on occasion may last three years or as little as six months.

Immature Stages

EGG. Up to 100 eggs are laid on or near a suitable larval food. They hatch in from 6 to 22 days according to temperature.

LARVA. Generally hairy. Distinctive tuft of very long hairs at the end of the abdomen. They moult from 6 to 20 times.

PUPA. Pupation occurs within the last larval skin and lasts from 5½ to 18 days. The adult remains immobile within the puparium for a period of from three to twenty days.

Carpet Beetle Attagenus pellio.
Length up to 5.7mm.

The genus *Anthrenus* is a most important one for those concerned with conservation of books. It consists of a number of small beetles from 1.5 to 4.0mm in length broadly oval in outline but much more nearly circular than in *Dermestes* and *Attagenus*. The body is strongly convex in outline dorsally and a distinctive feature is the dense covering of small scales of several contrasting colours giving a distinctive pattern. When at rest the short clubbed antennae lie in furrows or recesses under the prothorax. They are generally known as Carpet beetles (as also are species of *Attagenus*). The brown larvae are short compared with the long bodies of those of *Dermestes* and *Attagenus* but like them are covered with strong setae of different lengths. Some of the latter occur in bunches on each side of the hind abdominal segments, caudal tufts, and are distinctive in that the setae terminate in 'arrow' – or 'spear-heads'. The larvae are commonly known as 'woolly-bears' and a number of species are important pests in buildings especially households where woollens, carpets, skins etc., may be severely damaged, in museums where insect collections are commonly destroyed and in libraries where old leather-bound books may be damaged. An apparent common feature of the biology of this genus is the habit of the adults of congregating on flowers of certain families e.g. UMBELLIFERAE where they feed on pollen and nectar. It is thought that, at least in some species, viable eggs are laid only after such feeding.

The following species are of importance:

Anthrenus museorum L. Museum beetle.

Anthrenus verbasci L. Varied Carpet beetle.

Anthrenus scrophulariae L. Common Carpet beetle.

Anthrenus flavipes (LeC) *vorax* (Waterhouse) Furniture Carpet beetle.

Anthrenus fuscus (Olivier).

Anthrenus pimpinellae (Fabricius).

Anthrenus sarnicus (Moczkowski).

Anthrenus lepidus (LeC.)

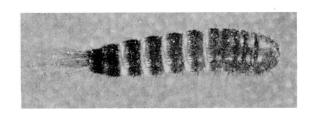

Larva of Carpet Beetle
Attagenus pellio.

85

MUSEUM BEETLE

Latin: *Anthrenus museorum*
American: *Lesser Museum beetle*
French: *Anthrene des musees*
German: *Museumkäfer*
Spanish: *Escarabajo de los museos*

Description of Adult Stage	A small anthrenid 2.0-2.8mm in length. The antennae are 8-segmented and the club is of two segments only. Yellow and white spotted similar to *A. verbasci* (except for antennae).
Distribution	Throughout Europe and North America but although occurring widely is not a serious pest in North America.
Time of Emergence	Not recorded.
Feeding Habits	In North America the larvae have been recorded as occurring in grain, wool, woollen articles, silk, museum specimens and dead Cluster flies, *Pollenia rudis*. It is reported occurring in birds' nests and dovecotes in Germany.
Type of Damage to Books	This species is not recorded as damaging books but its biology is such that it is likely to be concerned on occasion with its congeners.
Length of Life Cycle	At 18°C this is given as 10-11 months.
Immature Stages	EGG. Laid on the food substance and adhere to it and resist being dislodged by shaking. LARVA. The undersurface of the abdomen completely membraneous and the spear-headed hairs are neither prolonged nor thread-like. PUPA. Similar to other anthrenids.

VARIED CARPET BEETLE

Latin: *Anthrenus verbasci*
American: *Varied Carpet beetle*
French: *Anthrene des tapis*
German: *Wollkrautblutenkafer*
Spanish: *Escarabajo de las alfombras*

Description of Adult Stage

From 2-3mm in length. Dorsal surface clothed in white, brownish and yellow scales in irregular pattern but usually with two complete dark transverse bars and two incomplete. Antennal club is parallel-sided and consists of three segments and the eyes are smoothly rounded, i.e., not indented on inner side. Ventral surface covered with fine long greyish-yellow scale-like hairs.

Distribution

Listed as a British native insect but occurs as a household pest mostly in the South-east. Probably now occurs throughout North America but apparently especially common in California and as a troublesome household pest in Australia.

Time of Emergence

Adults most abundant from late March to early Summer.

Feeding Habits

A pest of woollen materials, carpets (where fitted and undisturbed for long periods), blankets and furnishing materials, insect collections.

Type of Damage to Books

Not specified but most probably typical anthrenid damage.

Length of Life Cycle

In temperate climates the life cycle is usually annual but may be from 7 to 14 months according to availability of a varied food supply.

Immature Stages

EGG. About 0.55mm in length and about 0.27mm in width. White in colour when first laid but later creamy. Roughish shell and short spines at one end. Usually hatches in from 17 to 18 days.
LARVA. Begins to feed immediately on hatching and moults from 5 to 16 times according to

87

temperature, humidity and amount and type of available food. It reaches a length of about 5mm and is transversely banded in dark and light brown. On each side of the terminal segments of the abdomen are three tufts of bristles each with a spear-shaped process at the apex. If the larva is menaced it can roll into a ball with the spear-head bristles erected and spreading in all directions. The length of the larval period varies from about 220 to 320 days but exceptionally it has been found to be almost two years. The larva can withstand long periods of starvation and wanders considerable distances in search of food. Both in California and England they are known to inhabit birds' nests in roofs of buildings where they feed on feathers, dried excrement and dead birds and from such locations they wander throughout the building where they infest woollen materials, edges of carpets etc.

PUPA. Pupation takes place within the larval skin and lasts from about ten to thirteen days. The adult remains quiescent within the puparium for several days before becoming active.

COMMON CARPET BEETLE

Latin: *Anthrenus scrophulariae*
American: *Common Carpet beetle, Buffalo moth, Buffalo bug*
French: *Anthrene*
German: *Teppichkäfer*
Spanish: *Escarabajo común de los tapetes*

Description of Adult Stage

About 3mm in length and typical anthrenid shape, it is generally blackish in colour with some white scales and orange scales chiefly around the eyes. The pattern of scaling is variable and is sometimes similar to that of *A. flavipes*. The antennae are eleven-segmented and the oval club is of three segments. The eyes are indented on the inner side.

Time of Emergence

The adults are to be found on a number of cream-coloured blossoms at the end of May and early in June.

Feeding Habits

Out of doors the adults feed on pollen and nectar in the flowers of a wide variety of plant species (and where copulation takes place). The larvae infest woollen carpets, especially important when they are tacked to the floor, and other woollen textiles, as well as a wide range of animal, and to a lesser extent plant materials. Feathers, leather, furs, hairbrushes, silks, mounted museum specimens and pressed plants are recorded as being infested by this species.

Type of Damage to Books

This has not been specified but leather-bound books are most at risk.

Length of Life Cycle

In the temperate world there is usually an annual life cycle but there appears to be a variation in the length of the life stages. In some circumstances the larval life can be as long as two years in buildings, where the nutrients required for completion of the life cycle have been lacking.

Immature Stages

EGG. The white egg has a projection at one end which assists in anchoring it. When laid on woollen material the egg may be caught by one or two fibres or it may be 'thrust so deeply into it that only one end is visible'. One female was observed to lay 36 eggs which hatched in 10 to 18 days.

LARVA. Reddish-brown covered with abundant black or brown hairs and from 2.5-3.5mm in length. Recorded as moulting six times and the larval period averaging 66 days at room temperature.

PUPA. Pupation takes place within the larval skin and lasts for from nine to nineteen days according to temperature. On emergence the adult lies quiescent within the puparium (the old larval skin) for approximately 18 days.

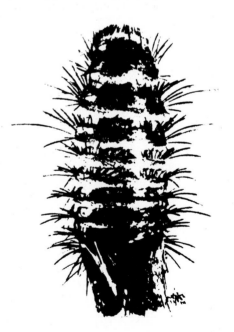

Larva of Varied Carpet Beetle
Anthrenus verbasci.

LEATHER EATER

Latin: *Anthrenus fuscus* (Olivier)

No common English name but translation of Russian name is 'Leather Eater'

Description of Adult Stage

Antennae are only 5-segmented, the last at least three times as long as the others united; longer in the male. The transverse bands on the lytra are yellow and the legs are red.

Distribution

This species, according to Kloet and Hincks (1945) is a British native species but is not included as a pest species in any British accounts. It is not cited as a pest species in North America but Kozulina (see Petrova 1953) states that *A. fuscus* is quite common in book collections in Moscow but less frequently than *A. museorum*.

Time of Emergence

Towards the end of March, reaching a peak between the end of April and the beginning of May but isolated individuals may emerge as late as July.

Feeding Habits

Apart from a diet consisting entirely on dried meat, unboiled animal glue and wheat-flour biscuits the larvae must subsist on a mixed diet of vegetable and animal substances in order to attain the adult stage. A 'wheat biscuit' diet alone however doubles the life cycle to two years. Natural silk, wool broadcloth, leather, dried insects as well as paper will serve the larvae as food, but only for a period. The larvae will survive for months on these foodstuffs singly but will not finally metamorphose into adults. The importance of hygiene in respect of food consumption in the library will be seen to be of paramount importance. A few crumbs dropped may provide all that is necessary to perpetuate an important book pest.

Type of Damage to Books

On leather bindings but also on paper-bound books with leather spines and corners as well as on book edges.

91

Immature Stages

EGG. Creamy-white, oval-shaped, 1.0-1.2mm in length and 0.50-0.55mm in width criss-crossed with streaks and stripes due to varying thickness of the shell. The shell is covered with bristles of varying lengths which serve to adhere to uneven surfaces and thus to attach the egg to its substrate. The average number of eggs laid under laboratory conditions was found to be 36-38. At 22°C and 69-70% Relative Humidity the eggs hatched in 12-15 days.

LARVA. When hatched the larvae keep together at first then disperse in all directions in search of food. The number of moults was 8-9 and took place either in fluff on the spine or on the back. At first the larvae are a 'dirty yellow' in colour with long hairs on the back and very small hairs underneath. There is a tuft of long hairs on each side of the first thoracic segments. These tufts, when the larva is resting, lie along the abdomen like short-haired brushes but when menaced the larva erects the brushes and the hairs fan out in a defensive attitude. A tuft of long hairs terminate the abdomen and during development of the larva these hairs become more numerous whereas the body hairs become comparatively shorter. The hard ring-like plates on the thoracic and abdominal segments become dark brown. The larval stage lasts for about 325 days under laboratory conditions (Kozulina). Amongst a collection of books, *Anthrenus* larva can find all that they require in diet to attain the adult stage and Kozulina found them in varied situations accompanied by book damage.

PUPA. This stage takes place within the larval skin and usually occurs at the end of February and during March and lasts about 8 days. Additionally the adult beetle remains within the larval/pupal skin for about 6 days. Kozulina states that *A. fuscus* is very widespread in libraries; it feeds on books and may find food elsewhere on the premises if these are not kept clean.

Other Species

The larvae of a number of other species of *Anthrenus*, *Attagenus* and *Dermestes* are known to feed on leather, hides and skin but are not specifically identified as attacking books. Several of them are uncommon or rare. In at least one case confusion has arisen as to almost certain mis-identifications in the past e.g. *Anthrenus sarnicus* which closely resembles *A. verbasci*.

The standards of book conservation have arisen enormously since the Second World War.

Anthrenus sarnicus *(a) Dark form as originally figured. (b) More usual light form (Rentokil collection)*.

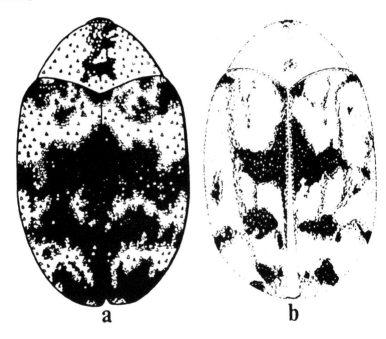

a   b

Reesa vespulae Milliron.

This dermestid is a new arrival in Britain having been first found in Essex, England in 1977. It is a North American species where it is a museum infesting insect and herbarium collections. It is reported as a domestic pest in California. The first record in Europe was in 1975 in Norway (but the infestation dated from 1960) and from Germany in 1974. It is well established in Iceland. It is thought that when found in herbaria and seed collections the larvae have been feeding on dead infesting insects or the latter have been a necessary food component. The species is parthenogenetic.

The adult is from 2.0-4.0mm in length and elongate-oval in shape similar to species of *Dermestes*. The head and pronotum are black. The elytra are dark brown at the base and along the mid-dorsal suture and light brown on the hind two-thirds and these two areas are not quite separated by a yellowish-brown crescentic bands.

It does not appear to have been recorded so far as a pest of books but conservators should be aware of it, know what it looks like and report it if found.

A new British Dermestid Reesa vespulae 2-4mm.

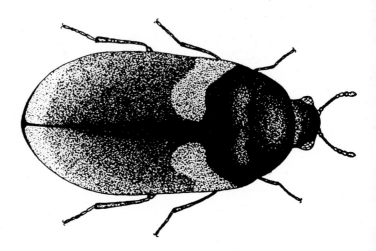

CHAPTER EIGHT

COLEOPTERA
Beetles
Anobiid beetles

The family ANOBIIDAE is made of up of well over a thousand species. They are mostly small, sombre-coloured and are generally characterized by the prothorax which is usually narrower at the front, sometimes has lateral extensions behind and mostly hoods over the head. The latter often appearing to be inserted almost vertically into the prothorax. The larvae are crescentic and the legs are small. The body is larger in the thoracic region and appears humped. The hinder abdominal segments are enlarged but nothing like to the extent as the thorax. A number of species are important wood borers causing much damage to structural timbers and furniture. Other species attack stored food products including flour and bread whilst such unusual materials as cigarettes and drugs (including opium) are not uncommonly infested by anobiid species. Several species are known to damage books.

Biscuit Beetle Stegobium paniceum. *Side view note that pronotum is flat not conspicuously convex as in* Anobium punctatum. *Red-brown. From 2-3mm in length.*

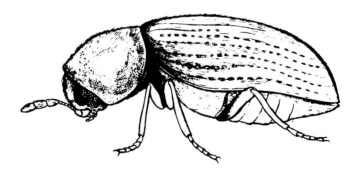

BREAD BEETLE
or
BISCUIT BEETLE

Latin: *Stegobium paniceum* (L.) At one time given the name of *Sitodrepa panicea*.
American: *Drug Store beetle*
French: *Vrillette du pain*
German: *Brotkäfer*
Spanish: *Carcoma del pan*

Description of Adult Stage

This is a small beetle usually only about 2.0mm in length and reddish-brown in colour. The pronotum is as wide as the wing-cases and completely masks the head when seen from above. The pronotum and the wing-cases are covered with fine hairs, those on the wing-cases are arranged in longitudinal rows. All margins are convex.

Distribution

This species is a cosmopolitan pest of a variety of farinaceous foods and various other cereal products, soup powders and dried materials of vegetable origin even poisonous substances (to human beings) such as strychnine.

Time of Emergence

As an indoors pest there does not appear to be a seasonal emergence.

Feeding Habits

Substances on which it feeds have been given above. The newly-hatched larva is active and wanders about for about eight days. It is very small only 0.5mm x 0.125mm in size, so that it can penetrate packaged foodstuffs usually with ease.

Type of Damage to Books

This is usually given as the larvae feeding on the dried flour paste on the back of the book but it is also known as feeding on the leather of book bindings. Damage to books is usually on the cover and adjacent leaves, the boreholes being parallel to the plane of the book. The diameter of the exit holes is between 1 and 2mm and are located on the binding and back.

Length of Life Cycle

As in all insects the length of the life cycle depends very much on temperature. At 17°C this is 200 days and at 26°C it is about 70 days.

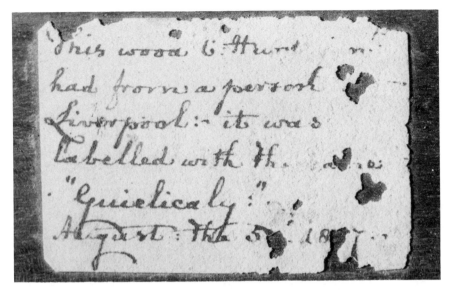

Paper label damaged by Silverfish Lepisma saccharina. *On right hand side damage to paper surface 'thinning' and removal of ink.*

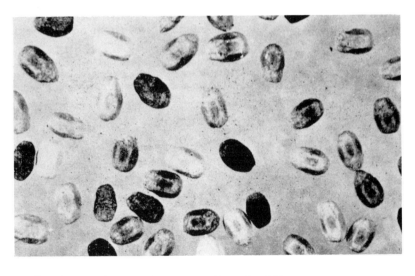

Faecal pellets of Drywood Termite. Note concave sides and seed-like appearance.

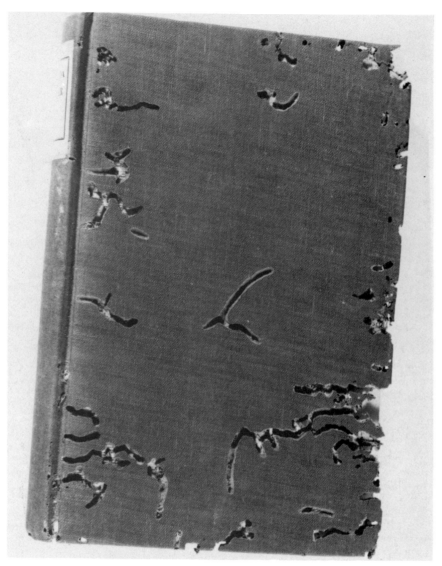

Above: Damage to book cover by Drywood termite Cryptotermes brevis. *The galleries are in longitudinal section the other half occupying the cover of the adjacent book. Diameter of galleries 2mm. Bermuda.*

Opposite: Leather-bound book attacked by Dry-wood termites. Galleries in leather allow termites to pass but passages into interior of book are only one termite wide. Nassau Bahamas.

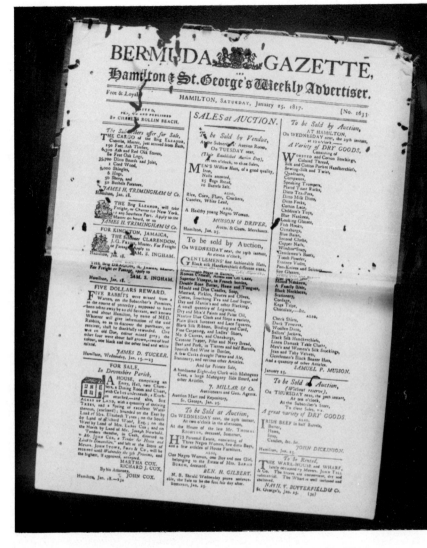

Above: Damage to inside of book by Drywood termite Cryptotermes brevis. *The end-papers of book illustrated in plate 3 show that galleries do not extend into the book. Bermuda.*

Opposite: Book destroyed by European Dampwood Termite Reticulitermes lucifugus *stained with faecal matter and mud.*

SENTA...

SUR LES A...TIO...

COMPRIS DAN... ...LES...

190

...LLOCATIO... AU R...CEPTEUR D... S...S REMISES ET FRA...

Government records stored for long periods are vulnerable. Complete destruction by termite Reticulitermes lucifugus.

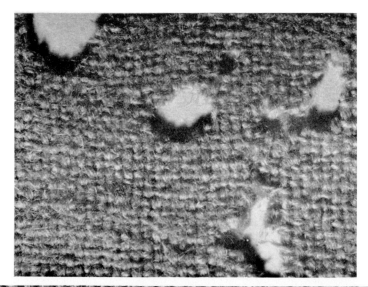

Top: Damage to woollen fabric by larva of Common Clothes Moth Tineola biselliella.
Bottom: adult moth, tunnels and faecal pellets.

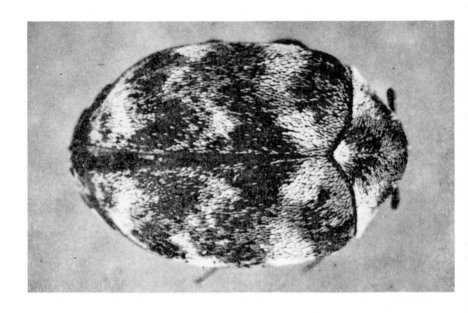

Top: Varied Carpet Beetle Anthrenus verbasci. *Variable pattern of white, brownish and yellow patches of scales. Length 2 to 3mm. Bottom: Larva.*

Damage to book by Biscuit Beetle. Galleries are mostly clean but faecal material packed into side chambers. Damage confined to flour paste on cotton or linen.

Above: Damage to book (1880) by Biscuit Beetle, Drugstore Beetle U.S.A. Damage confined to spine (back) and vicinity wher flour paste has been used on cotton or linen.

Opposite: Eggs of Common Furniture Beetle Anobium punctatum.

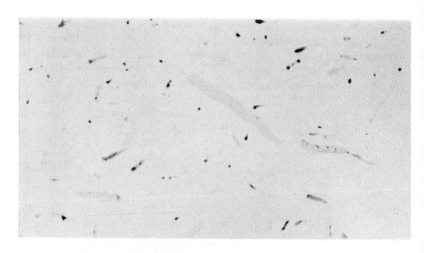

Top: Stains made by Oriental Cockroach Blatta orientalis *on paper.*

Bottom: Death Watch Beetle side view Xestobium rufovillosum.

Flight holes of Anobium punctatum *in vellum-covered book. Flight hole connects with pupal chamber at right-angles to the cover.*

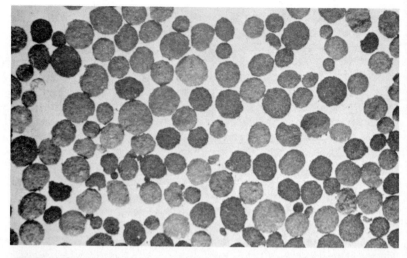

Above: Bun-shaped faecal pellets of Death Watch Beetle.

Below: Larva of Death Watch Beetle Xestobium rufovillosum *with 'bun-shaped' faecal pellets. A flight hole of adult is also shown.*

Book bored by Death Watch Beetle Xestobium rufovillosum. *In this example all galleries are at right-angles to the face of the book.*

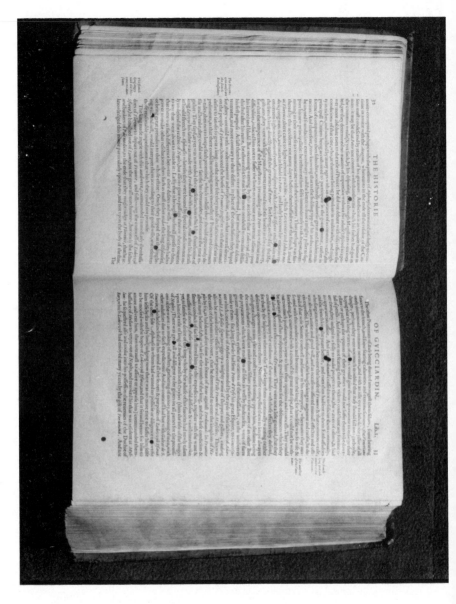

Book bored by Death Watch Beetle Xestobium rufovillosum. *All galleries pierce the book from side to side.*

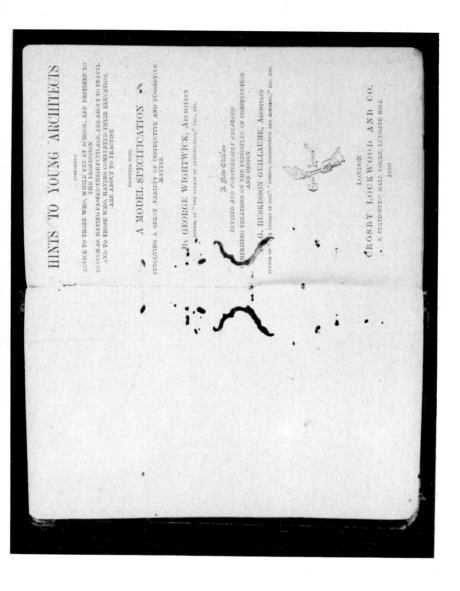

HINTS TO YOUNG ARCHITECTS

COMPRISING

ADVICE TO THOSE WHO, WHILE YET AT SCHOOL, ARE DESTINED TO THE PROFESSION

TO SUCH AS HAVING PASSED THEIR PUPILAGE ARE ABOUT TO TRAVEL

AND TO THOSE WHO, HAVING COMPLETED THEIR EDUCATION, ARE ABOUT TO PRACTISE

TOGETHER WITH

A MODEL SPECIFICATION

INVOLVING A GREAT VARIETY OF INSTRUCTIVE AND SUGGESTIVE MATTER

By GEORGE WIGHTWICK, ARCHITECT

AUTHOR OF "THE PALACE OF ARCHITECTURE," ETC., ETC.

A New Edition

REVISED AND CONSIDERABLY ENLARGED

COMPRISING TREATISES ON THE PRINCIPLES OF CONSTRUCTION AND DESIGN

By G. HUSKISSON GUILLAUME, ARCHITECT

AUTHOR OF "THE THEORY OF ART," "DESIGN, CONSTRUCTIVE AND ÆSTHETIC," ETC. ETC.

LONDON

CROSBY LOCKWOOD AND CO.

7, STATIONERS' HALL COURT, LUDGATE HILL

1880

*Damage to book by Biscuit
Beetle only reaches title page.
Does not usually damage
printed pages.*

Immature Stages

EGG. About 100 eggs are laid in and around the foodstuff during a period of approximately three weeks.

LARVA. Grows to about 5mm in length and is crescent-shaped, fat and sluggish when fully-grown. (See above under feeding habits for newly-emerged larva.) It is greyish or creamy-white in colour depending on foodstuff. The body is covered with minute bristles to which the powdered foodstuff adheres and probably help the larva in locomotion through such materials or through tight crevices.

PUPA. A pupal cell is constructed of food debris stuck together with saliva adjacent to the food material.

On emergence the adult bites its way out and can perforate a number of grades of paper in order to escape. It lives for about 6 to 8 weeks during which time it seeks a mate but does not eat.

Anobium punctatum *Length 2.5-4.5mm.*

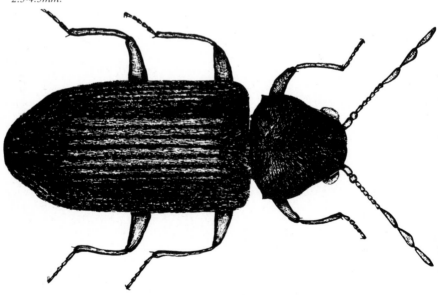

COMMON FURNITURE BEETLE

The larvae are generally known as 'Woodworm' although this term may be applied to the larvae of all species of wood-boring beetle found in buildings. *Anobium punctatum* (Degeer). At one time there was some confusion as to its correct scientific name. *Striatum* (Olivier) and *domesticum* (Geoffroy) have been used in older accounts. It seems strange that this insect appeared to be unknown to Linnaeus.

American: *Furniture Beetle*
French: *Petite vrillette du bois, Vrillette commune – larva: vers du bois*
New Zealand: *Houseborer*
Australia *Houseborer*
South Africa *Houseborer*
German: *Holzwurm*
Spanish: *Carcoma común de muebles*

Description of Adult Stage

This small beetle is variable in size from 2.5 to 5.0mm in length. The colour too, is rather variable according to age from light reddish yellow through dark chocolate brown to pitchy-red. Some of the variation in colour is due to the pubescence rubbing off. The legs are usually reddish-brown. The prothorax is narrower at the front and forms a hood over the head the latter appearing to be inserted vertically underneath. When viewed from above the head cannot be seen except for the eyes and antennae. The terminal three segments of the latter are enlarged. The elytra (wing-cases) show a series of 9 longitudinal rows of dark-coloured marks on each. These marks are areas of local thinning and are pit-like. The elytra are dilated somewhat at the apex. The wings are well-developed and the beetle is capable of sustained flight although afterwards the wings are not folded under the wing-cases as neatly as before and the wing tips are often visible.

The sexes can be identified by examining the abdomen from underneath. The 'telson', the apical sclerotized lobe that covers the genitalia from above, shows the apical margin sinuate in the female, whereas in the male it is strongly convex. In addition, the last visible sternite bears a depression in the case of the male which is absent in the female.

Distribution

Anobium punctatum is indigenous to the greater part of temperate Europe. It can be assumed that it is native also to temperature Asia. Becker (Berlin) states that it is the commonest and most destructive of the ANOBIIDAE of Central, North and East Europe. He goes on to say that the distribution is so extensive in Germany that it is possible to find the animal in nearly every building. Every kind of processed or other dead wood, of every kind of tree, used in any way at all, is attacked by it. It is known also from Russia, although its precise status as an economic pest is not known.

Stephens (1839) stated that *Anobium punctatum* was abundant in old houses throughout the country (England) and today it is certain that it is to be found in every parish in the United Kingdom. It has been estimated that three quarters of all buildings in Britain contain an infestation of this species most probably in the roof space but also in joinery and structural timbers. It is also a common insect out of doors attacking the dead parts of living trees such as where branches have been cut off, or situations where the bark has been removed thus killing the underlying sapwood.

The reason for the increased spread of infestations has been given as the increased mobility of the population. About three quarters of a million families change home every year – and they take their woodworm-infested furniture with them! It would appear that the insect is more prevalent in the west, the wetter side of Britain, than in the east.

In addition to Europe *Anobium punctatum* is to be found in a number of countries where there are temperate areas and which were colonized from Europe. As long ago as 1905 this insect was reported in New Zealand and since that time great damage has been done to buildings. The great majority of the latter are constructed of wood. Although there are native termite and Longhorn beetle species in New Zealand, by far the most important damage is caused by the Common House Borer as it is called there.

In North America it is widely distributed on the eastern side although it does not occur in such spectacular proportions. It is thought only to have been introduced about a hundred years ago.

In South Africa the insect was not noticed until 1939 but ten years later Tooke (1949) stated that it was widely distributed throughout all four provinces of the Union but the most serious and extensive damage was found in coastal areas.

It is not likely that *Anobium punctatum* will become a timber-pest in tropical areas in any continent except where altitude brings a more temperate climate.

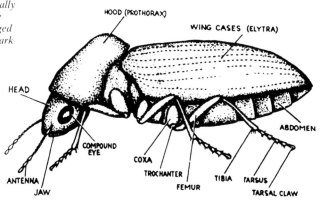

Anobium punctatum *Side view. Cowl-like pronotum, head inserted almost vertically downwards, terminal three segments of antenna enlarged and longitudinal rows of dark spots on wingcases. Dark brown. length 2.5-5.0mm.*

HOOD (PROTHORAX)

WING CASES (ELYTRA)

HEAD

ABDOMEN

COMPOUND EYE

COXA

ANTENNA

TROCHANTER

TIBIA TARSUS

FEMUR

JAW

TARSAL CLAW

101

It is not known when this wood-boring beetle was introduced into Australia but it is widespread throughout temperate areas. In New South Wales mainly softwoods are attacked and the timber of white pine, *Podocarpus dacrydioides* is specially mentioned but the incidence of attack in *Eucalyptus* and other hardwoods is comparatively slight. Heavy infestations have occurred in Tasmania. The timber of *Acacia melanoxylon* and White pine have been implicated.

Time of Emergence

In Britain the adults emerge generally about the third week of July but in centrally heated premises the emergence period is much extended. Indeed adults have been reported in every month of the year.

Feeding Habits

The chief larval food is the dead sapwood of a wide range of softwood tree species *Abies*, *Pinus*, *Podocarpus*, *Thuja*, *Picea*, *Larix* etc., followed by the heartwood when the sapwood has been widely tunnelled. The larvae feed also on the sapwood of hardwoods and then at a late stage in the infestation the heartwood is attacked. Linscott (1967) tested a large number of commercially available timbers and found only six timbers, all tropical hardwods, that were very resistant or immune to attack.

Type of Damage to Books

There are two types of damage. In the first place old books with wooden covers over which another material such as leather, vellum and velvet or some other textile is stretched and fixed. Secondly almost any type of book and of any age which is stored either on an infested shelf or on the infested floor. Indeed any situation where the book or books is in contact wsith woodworm-infested material. In the first type eggs may be laid on the book itself wherever there is a suitable crevice for insertion (see latter under EGG) and the whole of the life cycle would be passed in the wooden book covers and the flight holes shown as perfectly circular holes averaging 1.5mm in diameter.

102

In the second type it would be rare for eggs to be laid on the book itself and rare still for a complete life cycle to be passed within such books. That is not to say that extensive damage may not take place.

In both cases however damage by *Anobium punctatum* can be identified by:

1. The presence of the beetle itself in season. Identification of the larva when damage is severe and the infected part is broken up. Otherwise the larvae are never in view.
2. Examination of frass. Individuals pellets under X10 lens are pointed at each end.
3. Tunnels are always circular and flight holes on exterior surface similarly and not more than 2.0mm in diameter. Lacunae (broad excavated areas) absent.

Faecal pellets of Anobium punctatum. *Note general cylindrical shape and points at both ends when viewed with X10 lens.*

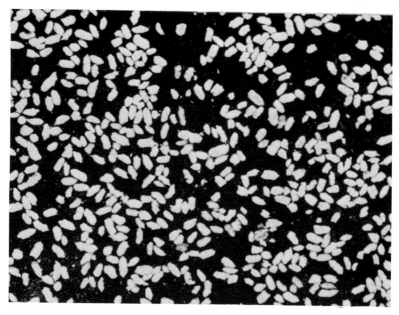

103

Length of Life Cycle	It is probable that out-of-doors Common Furniture beetle has an annual life cycle. Indoors however this period is an extremely variable one. At one time it was believed that two years was spent in development but later estimates reckon that perhaps three years was about average and that some larvae spend many years within dry furniture before emerging. In old book collections obviously much will depend on environmental conditions.
Immature Stages	EGG. Eggs of *Anobium punctatum* are about 0.35mm wide and 0.55mm in length. They are whitish and acorn-shaped. The egg-laying site is always a crack or crevice or very rough surface in which the egg can be partially wedged or anchored. Eggs are never laid indiscriminately on smooth surfaces or otherwise unsuitable surfaces except where the natural oviposition site is simulated in the laboratory. The normal egg-laying sites indoors are rough end-grain, rough-sawn timber and open joints between two pieces of wood and the rough edges of plywood. Most importantly, from the book-damage point of view eggs are laid at the joins between leather or textile and wood or in the near vicinity of wood. They are often in groups of two, three, or four. The female is capable of laying up to 80 eggs. It has been stated that 'under normal conditions' the eggs take from 'four to five weeks to hatch but Bletchly found that at 20°C and 87 per cent Relative Humidity the incubation period was 15.5 days but at 43 per cent Relative Humidity it was 23.3 days. Indoors in Britain in July/August it is likely to be longer.
LARVA. When the young larva eats its way out of the egg it does so through the base, i.e. at the rough bottom of the egg where yeast-like cells have been gathered from the oviduct of the parent. The yeast-like cells are taken into the gut and therafter live there and multiply and play an important part in the digestion of the cellulose the main constituent of wood. The larva thus bites its

104

way directly into the wood and the frass fills the empty egg-shell. The young larvae which are straight – not curved at this stage – can withstand a certain amount of starvation on leaving the egg.

The whole of the larval stage is spent in a gallery in the wood so that for examination it must be collected by cutting open the infested wood. The gallery or tunnel is made entirely by the mandibles of the larva. The larva is strongly arched when taken from the wood but this, of course, is not its normal shape in the wood but is brought about by the action of the strong abdominal muscles when the walls of the tunnel have been removed. The total length of the larva may be up to 7mm but the last three abdominal segments point towards the head. Except for the head the skin is soft and varies in colour from creamy-white through greyish-white to yellow. On occasion it may have a pinkish tinge. The head is light brownish-yellow with the sclerotized area around the mouth and the mandibles chestnut-coloured to black. There are six very small legs. Transversely the dorsal surface of the body is strongly curved whilst the ventral surface

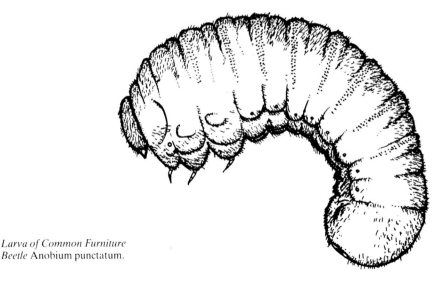

Larva of Common Furniture Beetle Anobium punctatum.

105

is flattened. Although the body is generally cylindrical the thoracic segments, the first two and the last three abdominal segments are enlarged. The whole surface of the head and body is covered with fine, erect, light golden-yellow setae. On the dorsal surface of the third thoracic and the first seven abdominal segments there is a band of small but strong spinules which have the function of holding the larva against the tunnel wall for locomotion.

The faecal pellets of the larva possess a characteristic shape being roughly cylindrical but pointed at both ends. This gives a 'gritty' feel when it is rubbed with a finger on the palm of the other hand.

When fully-fed the larva tunnels towards the outside of the wood, this part of the gallery often being straight. Before reaching the outside and breaking through the surface skin the gallery is widened to form a pupal chamber. The larva then turns round and constructs a thin diaphragm of wood fragments, closing the chamber at the tunnel end. It then takes up its original position in the chamber and then assumes a rather attenuated posture – the prepupal phase. The change to pupa then takes place by shedding the last larval skin.

PUPA. In the pupa the elytra, wings, legs, mouth parts, antennae and eyes of the adult can be made out but a thin soft cuticle envelopes the body and all the appendages. The pupa is immobile except that the last few abdominal segments can be moved. The pupa is milky-white at first and the whole integument is devoid of hair, setae and bristles being completely smooth. The eyes are the first to become pigmented, then the mandibles followed by the tarsal claws just before the metamorphosis, the adult colouring on the whole body can be seen immediately underneath the now completely transparent pupal cuticle.

The length of the pupal stage is between six and eight weeks although some investigators give shorter periods.

106

When the pupal cuticle has been ruptured the adult beetle remains for a time in the pupal chamber to allow the exoskeleton to harden. It then bores out of the wood making a circular flight hole 1.1-2.0mm in diameter (average 1.5mm). The latter is made by the mandibles of the adult whilst the beetle rotates on its axis.

A number of materials have been recorded as being perforated by the emerging adults of this species, the most important from a book point of view being leather. This is a well-known phenomenon. Thick cardboard is easily tunnelled by the larvae and by the adult beetles. This is often observed in framed pictures but the glass defeats them and the beetles become trapped.

DEATH WATCH BEETLE

Xestobium rufovillosum (Degeer 1774) but *tessellatum* (de Villers 1789) has been widely used. A number of other names have been used to a lesser extent but of these *pulsator* (Schall.), and *pulsatorium* (Scriba), are of special interest – see later.

American: *Death watch beetle*
French: *Horloge de la mort, Grosse vrillette*
German: *Totenuhr*
Spanish: *Escarabajo del Reloj de la muerte*

Death watch beetle is the largest species in the familiy ANOBIIDAE. It is of great interest not only on account of its biology but because of its historical significance. We can go back three centuries for an account of an insect whose identity can be established without question. The tapping noise, produced by the adults of both sexes was sufficiently distinctive to merit the attention of the seventeenth-century naturalists. The first writer was Swammerdam who wrote his 'History of Insects' sometime between 1637 and 1680. He describes the ticking noise made by a beetle which he called *Scarabeus sonicephalus*. The latter can be freely translated as 'head noises' so that Swammerdam was familiar with the mechanism by which the noise was produced.

Description of Adult Stage

This large anobiid is from 5 to 7mm in length. The prothorax is flanged laterally and extends to the width of the elytra. The head, as is usual in the ANOBIIDAE, is partially retracted into the prothorax and is normally held almost vertically downwards. In general the females are somewhat larger than the males but this cannot be relied upon to separate the sexes with certainty. The colour is dark chocolate brown to greyish-brown thickly 'tessellated' with yellowish scale-like hairs in small patches. However the yellow scales rub off a few days after emergence when the colour becomes more reddish.

108

Distribution	Death watch beetle occurs throughout Europe including Corsica. In Africa it is recorded from Algeria. As a native insect however it is absent both from Scotland and Ireland. In both countries it is known only from timbers imported from England. It is known also from the United States and Canada where it has been found in timbers originating in England. It is recorded from Russia where it is listed as a pest of old books.
Time of Emergence	The earliest appearance of Death watch beetle in an infested building in England is recorded as mid-March but the usual emergence occurs in the latter part of April and at the beginning of May. Generally emergence has finished in early June. There are records however of July beetles but these are quite exceptional. It must be made clear that 'Time of Emergence' used here as a subtitle indicates time of emergence from the wood through a flight hole. This distinction must be made because in this species change from pupa to adult takes place in Autumn but the beetle remains quiescent in the pupal chamber until the following Spring before boring its way out.
Feeding Habits	In nature the larva of this insect feeds on the partially rotted wood of broad-leaved trees. A common situation is in the crown of a pollard willow. However the reason for the widespread occurrence of Death watch infestation in old buildings in England is on account of the timber, oak, and chestnut, having been used in the construction of the building. In order to obtain the large dimensions required, wood was used containing a partially rotted pocket and already infested with Death watch. Thus Death watch was introduced into the building when it was originally constructed.
Type of Damage to Books	This is caused by books being placed adjacent to infested woodwork, either with the book upright or flat. In old buildings large-dimensioned oak

timbers were laid on the ground to serve as floor joists and the flooring nailed in position. In such situations the damp floor joists give ideal conditions for Death watch infestations shown by the parallel rows of flight holes in the flooring. Books stored directly in contact with the floor are obviously at great hazard. Books with wooden covers may harbour the larvae for a time but it would not be usual for such covers to be badly infested unless a fungal rot was present. The entire thickness of books, both lengthwise and across can be penetrated and flight holes between 4 and 5mm diameter in any position are made.

Length of Life Cycle

Over a period of many years Fisher attempted to correlate the length of life cycle of Death watch with the type and degree of fungal attack of oak sapwood and many interesting results were obtained. Within certain limits, the extent of the decay determined the length of the life cycle and consequently the rate of the disintegration of the wood due to the larval boring. With only slight decay (18 per cent loss in weight) the life cycle extended to 55 months but where it was severe (73 per cent loss in weight) the complete life cycle was passed through in less than 12 months and the wood was completely disintegrated by the tunnelling of the larva. However in some experiments the larvae took 10 years to complete the life cycle. Out of doors in oak attacked by the fungus *Phellinus cryptarum*, the life cycle varied from three to seven years.

Immature Stages

EGG. This measures in length about 0.65mm by 0.45mm at the greater width and is lemon-shaped but slightly more pointed at one end. When first laid it is pearly-white and at the top is a circular translucent patch. (The micropyle which later becomes more pronounced.) Shortly before hatching the egg becomes more opaque. Temperature and humidity have a considerable effect on the numbers laid. Generally between 40 and 60 eggs

110

are laid but between 39 and 201 have been recorded. Out of doors the length of the egg stage is about five weeks. Under laboratory conditions Fisher found that at 14.5°C the average incubation period was 35.7 days whilst at 18.3°C it was 25.2 days. No eggs hatched at low humidity (23 per cent) nor at low temperature (10°C).

LARVA. When first hatched from the egg the young larva is active, walking over the wood surface searching for a suitable crevice into which it burrows. The fully-grown larva is fleshy, soft and curved with six small legs. The thorax is swollen as are the last three abdominal segments but the latter not to the same extent as the former. The body is completely covered with longish, erect, golden-yellow setae and there are areas of spinules on the third thoracic and the first eight abdominal segments and in addition they occur at the sides and underneath of the ninth and tenth abdominal segments. An important feature for recognition of this species is the frass which contains large bun-shaped pellets. The total length of the larva is up to 11mm.

OTHER ANOBIIDS

Several other species of the family ANOBIIDAE are known to damage books but whilst not appearing to cause injury to books on a widespread scale nevertheless have caused damage to such an extent that they must be recorded in this account.

Neogastrallus librinocens (Fisher). This species was reported by Back in 1939 as causing damage to books in Florida. The books originated in Havana, Cuba, and apparently the beetle came with them. It is however recorded by Watson in 1943, from Florida and from Louisiana. The beetle is dark reddish-brown covered with a fine greyish hair. It measures 2.4mm in length and 1.2mm in width. The larva is whitish and from 2 to 3mm in length, when fully grown tunnels into books making galleries slightly more than 1mm in diameter. All books, old and new may be infested and the tunnels cut through the binding materials

111

causing the pages to fall out. The pages themselves may also be tunnelled and cut in construction of the pupal chambers.

Nicobium hirtum (Ill.). Is a native of Southern Europe but now established in the southern states of the United States. It is not known from Britain. Although normally a woodborer it is recorded by Herrick (1936) as damaging books in the Louisiana State Library in Baton Rouge.

Catorama bibliothecarum (Poeg.). Taylor (1928) records a tropical anobiid as attacking a stack of books brought to Boston, U.S.A. from Honolulu. It is probably this species as Back (1939) mentions it in his paper.

Catorama herbarium Mexican Book beetle. This species has been introduced into the United States where it is also injurious to seeds, furniture, leather, chocolate and Cayenne pepper.

THE CIGARETTE BEETLE

Lasioderma serricorne (F.). This species is listed by Back (1939) as a pest of books in the United States. It is best known as a tobacco pest and occurs throughout the world wherever tobacco is grown, cured or manufactured. In addition however it is known to be injurious to seeds and spices and similar dried vegetable material.

Howe (1957) states that *Lasioderma serricorne* has probably the most varied taste in food of all storage insects. It is recorded as damaging leather, paper, books and book-binders paste.

Description of Adult Stage

When viewed from the side this beetle has an uninterrupted rounded profile unlike *Stegobium paniceum* where the division between prothorax and wing cases is marked. Otherwise *L. serricorne* is somewhat similar to *S. paniceum* but has a more squat appearance and is a little smaller. It is about 2 to 3mm in length and is reddish-brown in colour with no conspicuous rows of dark marks on the wing-cases as are present in *S. paniceum* and *Anobium punctatum*.

Distribution

Cosmopolitan as given above.

Time of Emergence

Independent of season in warm climates but in north temperate regions the first emergence is in May then usually again in August.

Feeding Habits

The young larva is active whilst searching for foodstuff and can survive starvation for about a week but then becomes fleshy and immobile. A cell is constructed of food fragments in which pupation takes place. Development ceases below 21°C.

Type of Damage to Books

The type of damage has not been described but it is probable that this species damages books only in warmer environments. It is reported as damaging books neither in Britain nor in Russia.

Length of Life Cycle

This has been well-studied in relation to the tobacco trade especially by Bovingdon (1931). In warm regions the total life cycle lasts usually from

70 to 90 days but may be longer in temperate areas giving an annual life cycle.

Immature Stages

EGG. Several investigators give different data obviously varying with climate conditions. 30 to 100 eggs are laid in crevices and folds of the potential food material over a period from one week to three. The incubation period is from six to ten days.

LARVA. The young larva resembles that of *Stegobium paniceum* in that it is at first active and can survive starvation in its first week whilst it finds the foodsource. It then becomes curved and fat and spends from 5 to 10 weeks in this stage. It has been found feeding on a wide variety of dried vegetable matter although tobacco is preferred.

PUPA. The pupal stage is passed in a chamber made of food debris and lasts from 7 to 42 days. Severe infestations have been recorded when the number of beetles swarming was so vast that they caused considerable distress by getting into the hair and the clothes.

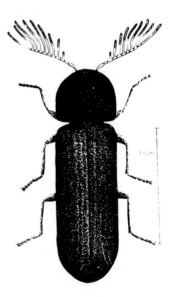

Ptilinus pectinicornis. *The unmistakable feathery antennae are only possessed by the male. 3mm.*

Ernobius sp. There is a reference to two unnamed species of this genus damaging books in Moscow (Petrova, 1953), but no further information appears to be available. Identification of the species of this genus is difficult. Eight species are described by Schwenke (1974) and outline drawings are given of six of them (Dominik 1955).

Ernobius mollis is a common British species in buildings where softwood structural timber is attacked. However this occurs only where the bark has not been removed, the tunnelling takes place between the outer sapwood and the inner bark. The infestation dies out if the bark is removed. No references to damage to books by this species in Britain has been found.

Ptilinus pectinicornis is a dark-brown anobiid from 3 to 7mm in length. It is cylindrical in shape with the globular prothorax. The male is easily identified by the remarkable feather-like antennae whereas those of the female are merely saw-like. The larva bore into the wood of beech, maple, ash and sycamore and infestations are sometimes mixed with those of *Anobium punctatum*. The flight holes however are somewhat larger than those of the latter species but not as large as those of *Xestobium rufovillosum*. The bore dust is fine and silky to the touch, unlike that of *Anobium punctatum*.

Its importance to the librarian lies in its wood destroying larvae but it would appear to be much more common in Germany and Central Europe than it is in Britain. It occurs in North America but is reported to be of little economic importance as it only damages wood out-of-doors such as gate posts.

CHAPTER NINE

COLEOPTERA

Beetles
Ptinid beetles

The beetle family PTINIDAE is made up of about 500 species world-wide of which about 20 species are in the British list. At least five of the latter however (possibly more) have been introduced through commerce. This family and the ANO-BIIDAE are closely related. Most of the species are known as 'Spider' beetles due to a pronounced constriction between the prothorax and the mesothorax together with their relatively long legs giving a superficial resemblance to a spider. Ptinid beetles are small, rarely exceeding 5mm in length and, with few exceptions, are globular in shape and the prothorax is, in many, but by no means all, cowl-like hiding the head if viewed from above, except for the eleven-segmented thread-like antennae. The importance of the PTINIDAE to Man lies in the fact that many species are pests of habitation, infest stored food products, and do considerable damage to a wide range of vegetable and animal products associated with Man e.g. stored foodstuffs, drugs, textile and zoological and botanical specimens, as well as books.

In some accounts of book damage, the actual species of *Ptinidae* have not always been identified so that in this account the species *Ptinus tectus* has been described in addition to *Niptus hololeucus* and *Ptinus fur*.

116

GOLDEN SPIDER BEETLES

Latin:	*Niptus hololeucus* (Falderman)
American:	*Yellow* or *Golden Spider Beetle*
French:	*Ptine doré*
German:	*Messingkäfer*
Spanish:	*Escarabajos Araña*

Description of Adult Stage

This species varies from 3 to 4.5mm in length and is golden yellow in colour and covered in long, silky hairs. The prothorax and the remainder of the body covered by the wing cases are both globular, the former much smaller than the latter and this gives the appearance of a 'waist'. The prothorax completely hides the head from view when seen from above except for the long eleven-segmented thread-like antennae. The legs are relatively long. It cannot fly and can crawl only slowly.

Distribution

It is recorded from the whole of the temperate world.

Time of Emergence

Most plentiful in June and July.

Feeding Habits

It is not usually a pest of stored food products but most commonly occurs as a vegetable- and animal-debris feeder in warehouses and badly-maintained store-rooms. The adults browse on a number of different materials, often biting holes in garments, bedding and carpets.

Type of Damage to Books

The damage to books recorded by Petrova 1947-1949 by ptinid beetles is given as being similar to that caused by *Stegobium paniceum*. In stacked books the ptinid larvae were mostly found on the outside of the binding between two adjacent books. When standing on shelves however the larvae were usually found on the flyleaf and tunnels had been bored both towards the binding and towards the leaves. The development of this ptinid infestation had not been hindered by the low temperatures of several winters (Moscow).

| Length of Life Cycle | At normal temperatures an annual life cycle probably takes place but at 15°C it is about 300 days and at 18-20°C it is about 185 days. The adults are known to live as long as 250 days and are active down to 5.°C. |

Immature Stages

EGG. Ptinid eggs are whitish and often have a sticky coat to which adhere particles of foodstuffs and rubbish. Eggs of *Niptus hololeucus* vary in length from 0.6-0.8mm and in breadth from 0.4-0.5mm. Length of egg stage 15°C 20-30 days at 18-20°C from 11-20 days.

LARVA. The larva is whitish and curved with the hinder end of the abdomen curled vertically. When walking on a plane surface progress is made very slowly with the abdomen dragging along in the same line as the thorax. When disturbed it rolls up into a tight ball. The legs are relatively small but each bears a large curved claw. Length of larval life at 15°C about 250 days at 18-20°C about 150 days.

PUPA. Pupation takes place in a silk-lined chamber to which adheres debris of various kinds. Length of pupal stage at 15°C between 18-22 days. At 18-20°C about 18-22 days.

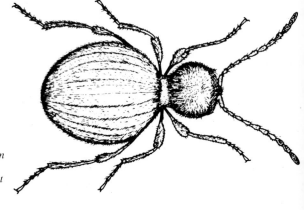

Golden Spider Beetle Niptus hololeucus. *Globular abdomen and prothorax distinctly waisted, head not visible except for long antennae. Wing cases covered with long golden hair. Length 3-4.5mm.*

AUSTRALIAN
SPIDER BEETLE

Latin: *Ptinus tectus* (Boieldieu)
American: *Australian Spider Beetle*
French: *Ptine velu*
German: *Australischer Diebkäfer*

Description of
Adult Stage

This insect may be from 2.5 to 4.0mm in length and has the wing covers clothed with brown or golden hairs giving a uniform fulvous colour so that the longitudinal rows of small dark marks are made invisible. The prothorax hoods over the head and the waist between it and the rest of the body is well shown. At the front of the prothorax is a small groove. The author reared many thousands of these insects and only once was any attempt to fly observed. It ran about in an excited manner and after arriving at the highest point of a piece of paper it opened its wing-cases and spread its wings. After a slight pause it lost its balance, toppled over, folded its wings then covered them with the wing-cases and became quiescent. All adults readily feign death when disturbed and shun the light (as do the larvae until a pupal chamber is constructed). Adults readily drink water, plunging their mandibles into a drop of water when found. A characteristic shared with other ptinids is the resistance to cold shown by both larvae and adults. Larvae and adults exposed to −8°C recovered after twelve hours at 15°C. The larvae developed into adults, and the adults laid eggs.

Distribution

Originating from Tasmania or Australia it was first recorded in Europe about 1900 but has since become a pest throughout the temperate regions of the world.

Time of Emergence

Early Summer.

Feeding Habits

A very wide range of dried vegetable and animal substances have been recorded as providing food for this species.

119

Type of Damage to Books	Similar to that caused by *Stegobium paniceum*.

Length of Life Cycle

A large number of rearing experiments were carried out by the present author using *Ptinus tectus*. Using standard materials the shortest average length of life cycle was 10.5 weeks which occurred in wholemeal flour in equilibrium with 60 per cent Relative Humidity at 27°C. The longest average length of life cycle was 36 weeks which occurred in casein in equilibrium with Relative Humidity of 80 per cent at 20°C. In a number of different foodstuffs the average length of life cycle was about twice as long at 20°C than at 27°C. When however, yeast powder was added to casein the shortest life cycle of all was found. It was eight weeks, when in equilibrium with 60 per cent Relative Humidity at 20°C. This food material also gave the highest number of reared adult progeny per parent female.

Immature Stages

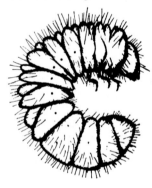

Larva of Australian Spider Beetle Ptinus tectus.

EGG. Whitish with slight opalescence, length from 0.47 to 0.55mm and breadth 0.29-0.40mm. Sticky when laid and fragments of debris soon adhere. Up to 120 eggs may be laid by a single female. The egg stage lasts from 3-16 days at 20-25°C.
LARVA. Typical ptinid shape and colour. This stage lasts from about 40 days to 4 or 5 months according to temperature and Relative Humidity.
PUPA. In the experimental work mentioned above the shortest average length of pupal life was 11.0 days and the longest 16.1 days. However the callow adult remains in the cocoon for some days before emerging. This was found to be from 6 to 11 days whatever the conditions.

BROWN SPIDER BEETLE

Latin: *Ptinus hirtellus* (Sturm.) In some accounts the names *Ptinus testaceus* (Olivier) and *Ptinus brunneus* (Duftschmid) have been used.

American: *Brown Spider beetle*

Description of Adult Stage

This ptinid is from 2.3 to 3.2mm in length and is uniformly brown in colour. It resembles *Ptinus fur* in appearance. The female is larger than the male and the body is egg-shaped and the antennae more robust. The legs of the male appear more 'spidery'.

Distribution

Generally considered to be cosmopolitan but is mostly found in the North Temperate zone where it often occurs along with *Ptinus fur* and may hybridise with it.

Time of Emergence

This may extend over a long period according to the conditions in its indoor environment.

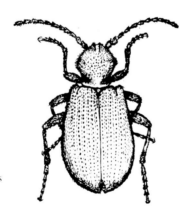

Australian Spider Beetle Ptinus tectus. *2.5-4.0mm.*

121

| Feeding Habits | This insect is a general scavenger in situations of minimal human disturbance such as cellars, attics and storehouses. The larvae have been recorded as feeding on feathers, skins, dried mushrooms, rat and mouse droppings, dried vegetable matter of various sorts as well as on books (in the United States). |

Type of Damage
to Books

The type of damage does not apear to have been recorded but is likely to be typically ptinid, i.e. the fully-fed larva burrowing into the covers in order to construct the pupal chamber.

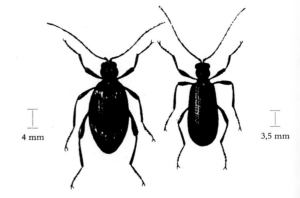

4 mm

3,5 mm

White-marked Spider Beetle
Ptinus fur. *2.0-4.3mm*

122

WHITE-MARKED SPIDER BEETLE

Latin: *Ptinus fur* (fur = thief)

Description of Adult Stage

From 2.0 to 4.3mm in length, in general appearance like a spider with long spindly legs. Body is reddish-brown covered with fine yellow hairs. There is a patch of pale hairs on the prothorax on each side near the base. The female has two white patches on each wing-case somewhat variable in intensity. The male is more longate than the female and lacks the white patches.

Distribution

Probably found throughout the North Temperate zone.

Time of Emergence

Throughout the year, adults recorded active in winter.

Feeding Habits

A general pest in warehouses, granaries, food-processing factories, museums and libraries where it can maintain itself under very cold conditions and the larvae browse on a wide variety of commodities and packaging.

Type of Damage to Books

Not recorded in detail but habit of larva of boring through cartons, sacks etc. immediately before pupation, would constitute a danger to stored books.

Length of Life Cycle

Howe and Burges, who made an extensive series of studies on the biology of ptinid beetles found that the optimum conditions for development were 73-4°F 23°C and 70 per cent Relative Humidity and that in these conditions the life cycle is completed in 32.1 days in fish meal. In Washington D.C. complete life cycle was found to take three and a half months. In the U.S.A. however, in general, in artificially heated buildings, it is thought that there are two life cycles annually.

123

HUMP SPIDER BEETLE

Gibbium psylloides (up to 3.2mm) is an atypical ptinid of curious appearance. It is nothing like *Ptinus tectus* in appearance being shining blood-red in colour and the fused elytra are strongly convex. It walks very slowly and it looks like a large mite. It is known to damage paper, wool and leather and is considered by Cymorek (1977) to be a book pest. It feeds on debris and residues of various sorts but is something of an enigma in that from time to time it appears in large numbers in buildings for no apparent reason. The adult is long-lived.

Under laboratory conditions complete life cycles were passed in wholemeal flour, plain flour and rice flour at 27°C and at Relative Humidity of 40 and 60 per cent. The length of the life cycle varied from 26 to 34 weeks with a mixed diet however and at 91.4°F the life cycle has taken only 45 days.

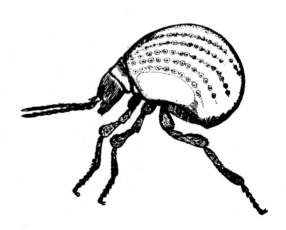

Hump Spider Beetle Gibbium psylloides.

CHAPTER TEN

BROWSERS and SPOILERS

Cockroaches and Crickets

A number of insect species, in certain circumstances, can cause harm to books in a general sense. This is not because books provide any nourishment for them but the very numbers that irrupt when swarms are produced cause widespread fouling and a browsing effect on all soft surfaces with which their mouthparts come into contact. This is particularly important in tropical and subtropical areas but on occasion occurs in warm temperate climates. Cockroaches and Crickets are important in this respect.

THE COCKROACH

Cockroaches are insects classified in the suborder BLATTARIA. They are joined with suborder MANTODEA – the mantids – to form the order DICTYOPTERA. Cockroaches are usually fairly large or large and robust and have large eyes and long whip-like antennae. The pronotum is large and shield-shaped and can usually cover the head. There are two pairs of wings, the forewings known as tegmina (singular tegmen) are leathery whilst the hindwings are membraneous. When alarmed cockroaches prefer to scurry rapidly into dark crevices which their flatness enables them to do rather than to fly. The ovipositor is not visible.

Eggs are laid in groups in a leathery capsule known as an ootheca. It is characteristic of many species that the female carries the half-extruded ootheca around with her when foraging for food etc. The young nymphs when hatched resemble the adults except for size and the absence of wings. The latter develop as flap-like buds at a late stage in the nymphal growth. Cockroaches are usually brown or drab in colour.

Cornwell (1968) states that the cockroach is probably the most obnoxious insect known to man. It is a world-wide pest and is regarded with loathing and abhorrence. This is on account of their rapid movement when alarmed together with their large size, very large numbers and their disagreeable tainting odour and fouling excrement.

ORIENTAL COCKROACH
(Black Beetle)

Latin: *Blatta orientalis* (Linnaeus)

A large cockroach, 20-24mm in length. Dark reddish-brown to nearly black. Wings of male almost reach apex of abdomen but tegmina of female stunted and hind wings either absent or very small. Neither sex flies. This species unable to climb up smooth surfaces due to absence of pad (arolium) between the claws.

Believed to have originated in North Africa it is now a major pest in all temperate climates throughout the world but has not become established in the humid tropics appearing to prefer rather cooler conditions than *B. germanica*. It does however favour situations in the near vicinity of water and often below ground level. Sometimes is able to survive out of doors both in Europe and North America. In the United States this species is commonly found in sewers and in ship's holds.

Common Cockroach Blatta orientalis *A. Mature male. B. Mature female. C. Female bearing egg-case. D. Last stage nymph.*

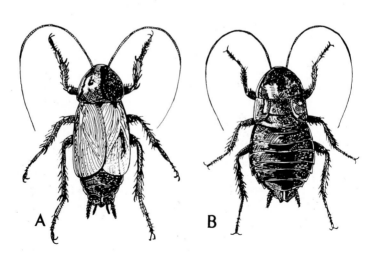

126

GERMAN COCKROACH
(Steamfly)

Latin: *Blattella germanica* (Linnaeus)

German Cockroach
Blattella germanica *Carrying egg-case.*

A small cockroach, 10-15mm in length. Ground colour pale ochraceous buff to tawny with dark parallel bands down the pronotum. In the nymph the bands are broader and continue onto the meso- and metanota.

Believed to have originated in N.E. Africa now found throughout Europe and is an important pest in the United States, Canada and Australia and is found in most parts of the world in buildings where warm, moist conditions prevail. It is rarely found out of doors in Britain. Likely to spill over from situations such as unhygienic bakeries, food manufacturing premises and such like. The librarian must look further than his own building especially in tropical and subtropical climates.

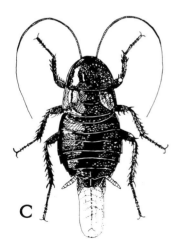

C

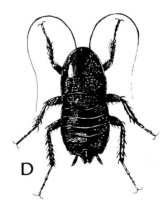

D

AMERICAN COCKROACH

Latin: *Periplaneta americana* (Linnaeus)

A large cockroach, 28-44mm in length. Shining reddish-brown with pale creamy-yellow edge around the pronotum. In the male the tegmina extend beyond the abdomen but in the female they just overlap the abdomen. They rarely fly and then in a clumsy manner.

It is thought to originate in tropical Africa. Stated by Cornwell (1968) to be an outstanding pest in tropical and sub-tropical areas and has been distributed by commerce throughout the lower latitudes and well into the temperate regions of most of the world, throughout almost the whole of India. Nigam (1933) states that this species infests every dwelling house, in the store-rooms, kitchens, cupboards and libraries, etc. In the United Staes, although most abundant in the southern states it is well-established in New York. In Britain it occurs in suitable industrial premises in extensive areas around ports.

The American cockroach like the German cockroach is mostly found in a warm moist environment.

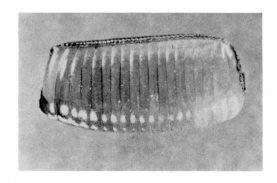

Egg-case of German Cockroach Blattella germanica *8mm in length.*

AUSTRALIAN COCKROACH

Latin: *Periplaneta australasiae* (Linnaeus)

A large cockroach, 30-35mm in length. It is reddish-brown in colour and the wings are fully developed and are longer than the tip of the abdomen in both sexes. It flies well. Like the American cockroach there is a creamish coloured edge to the pronotum which is rather more conspicuous in the present species.

The two species can be separated easily by the presence of a pale area at the basal margin of the tegmina *P. australasiae* probably originated in tropical Africa. It is now an important pest in buildings in many tropical areas of the world and extends into temperate regions where it has been introduced into heated buildings. This species requires a moist climate similar to *P. americana* although preferring a somewhat higher temperature. In Britain it has occurred a number of times in cargoes from the West Indies and Brazil.

BROWN COCKROACH

Latin: *Periplaneta brunnea* (Burmeister)

A large cockroach 31-37mm in length but smaller than *P. americana* which it greatly resembles in general appearance but the blotches on the pronotum are less conspicuous. It can fly in a gliding manner. It is thought to be native to Africa and its present distribution as a pest species is rather more confined to tropical regions than is *P. americana*. It is however, now an important pest in the southern States of the United States and is an obnoxious household pest and collected from army camps, city dumps, privies and sewers (Edmonds 1957).

BROWN-BANDED COCKROACH

Latin: *Supella supellectilium* (Serville)

A small cockroach, 13-14.5mm in length. Tegmina of male cover the abdomen but those of female rarely do so. The pronotum is dark in colour with the sides transparent but the latter may be absent. Adjacent to the pronotum there is a light moon-shaped area on the tegmina and the front margins are pale also with two pale blotches at the widest part. The ground colour is variable but usually reddish-brown. The nymphs, in the absence of the tegmina have two brown bands. It flies well.

It originated in Africa where it is an important pest north of the equator. In the New World it was recorded from Cuba in 1862 and since then has become established southwards to Brazil and throughout the southern half of the United States and there is scarcely a state in which it has not been recorded. So far it has been reported only a few times in Britain.

Its habitats differ from those of the German cockroach in that it hides high up in rooms, such as behind pictures, in drawers of furniture and cupboards. Mallis says that it is the commonest species in bedrooms in the United States. It is often found behind books on bookshelves and damages books by feeding on gum sizing and paste.

SMOKY-BROWN COCKROACH

Latin: *Periplaneta fuliginosa* (Serville)

This resembles *P. brunnea* in size being 31-35mm in length and in colour, although not quite so dark as *B. orientalis* it is shining almost black with brownish tints. In both sexes the wings are fully developed and cover the abdomen. It flies to light. Its origins are obscure but it is a common pest in the southern States of the United States. It is predominantly a sub-tropical species where it occurs out of doors but it is found indoors in Illinois and Iowa.

CRICKETS

Crickets are members of the family GRYLLIDAE in the order ORTHOPTERA which also includes the Grasshoppers and Locusts.

There are over 10,000 described species in the ORTHOPTERA of which the GRYLLIDAE make up about one thousand. We are concerned here however, with only two species.

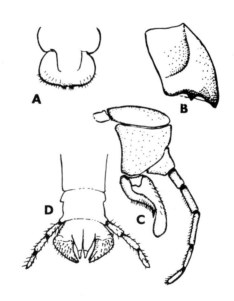

Mouthparts of a Cricket dissected.
(a) Labrum (upper lip)
(b) Mandible one of a pair.
(c) Maxilla with palp, one of a pair.
(d) Labium with palps (lower lip).

HOUSE CRICKET, EUROPEAN HOUSE CRICKET

Latin: *Gryllulus domesticus* (Linnaeus)
American: *House Cricket*

A medium sized insect, 18-20mm in length and light yellowish-brown in colour mottled in different tones. The antennae are long and thread-like and composed of thirty segments. They are well-known for their habit of jumping, the femora of the hind legs being conspicuously enlarged and muscular. Two pairs of wings are present, the forewings being toughter than the membraneous hindwings which fold up fanwise beneath them. The forewing of the male bears a serrated edge which comes into contact with a ridge or scraper on the other wing. The chirruping of the cricket is produced by raising the wings to about 45° with the abdomen and moving them so that the scrapers rub against the serrated edges. The sound is amplified by vibratory 'tympana' situated elsewhere on the wing. Two long cerci are present. The female possesses a long ovipositor.

The House cricket occurs indoors throughout the world and often takes up residence in rubbish dumps during the summer months. At times they invade adjacent buildings in vast numbers when they will gnaw holes in thin fabrics, cotton, silk, nylon, rayon, woollens as well as paper.

FIELD CRICKET

Latin: *Gryllus assimilis* F.
American: *Field Cricket*

This species is larger and stouter than the European House Cricket. The head and pronotum are almost black in colour but there is some variation in the intensity of the ground colour. The extremities of the hindwings extend backwards 'like pointed tails' and the cerci are very long.

In the New World it occurs widely in North America Central America and the northern parts of South America elsewhere it ocurs in tropical Asia. It would appear to require a higher temperature than the European House Cricket. It does not occur in Britain.

This species is a pest of field crops but when swarms invade buildings (believed to occur mainly when heavy rain follows a period of drought) great damage is often reported to a wide range of materials including garments, plastic fabrics, wood, leather and paper. Their potential danger to libraries is thus apparent.

Hibernation takes place in the egg stage, the eggs being buried from 5 to 25mm beneath the soil.

Field Cricket Gryllus assimilis. *Black head and pronotum, very long antennae. Long hind legs with thick femora. Pair of long abdominal cerci and female with long ovipositor. Length from head to end of extended back legs about 32mm.*

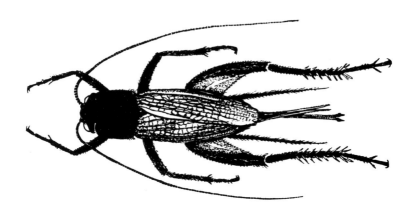

CLUSTER FLIES
(Swarming Flies)

Several species of the order DIPTERA,. the two-winged flies, are known as cluster flies from their habit of 'clustering' together in large numbers during hibernation. This often takes place in buildings, especially the upper floors of old buildings, where it has been traditional for many years for the clusters to occur. They enter buildings usually in September and October and aggregate together forming a tight ball during cold weather, sometimes as big as a tennis ball but often much larger. During warm spells they tend to disperse and bumble about the room but coming together again when the weather cools. They disperse in the Spring but many die during the Winter and it is for this reason that they are included here as being indirectly injurious to books. This is because their dead bodies provide food for dermestid beetle larvae. Indeed such high-protein diet is essential for completion of development of these book-damaging pests. However, large numbers of the flies cause a considerable amount of fouling by their depositing spots of dark-coloured faecal fluid which could harm books if placed near windows.

Cluster flies are found widely in Europe and North America except for the states bordering on the Gulf of Mexico. Two species common to both regions are *Pollenia rudis* (F.) in the family MUSCIDAE and the Raven Fly known in the U.S.A. as the Face Fly. *Musca autumnalis* (De. G.). *P. rudis* is somewhat larger than the Common House Fly *Musca domestica* (L.) but is stouter and when at rest the tips of the wings coincide whereas in *M. domestica* they diverge. In addition the longitudinal dark bands on the thorax of *Musca domestica* are absent in *Pollenia rudis* or only scarcely discernible.

In Europe another dipterous species commonly found in clusters usually together with *P. rudis* and *M. autumnalis* is *Thaumatomyia notata* in the CHLOROPIDAE. A few other species occur in these clusters rather more rarely.

The larval stage of *P. rudis* is parasitic within the body of a species of earthworm *Allolophora chlorotica* which explains its abundance around ancient buildings which are usually surrounded by the rich soil of old gardens and stables. The larval stage of *M. autumnalis* is passed in cattle and horse dung. Large swarms of *P. rudis* give off a sweet rather sickly smell said to resemble 'Buckwheat honey'.

Thaumatomyia notata is a small fly, yellow in colour with black marks. Its life cycle is unknown but it occasionally swarms in extraordinary numbers.

Cluster Fly Pollenia rudis. *Clusters, usually of many hundreds of the flies hibernate in older buildings. Their dead bodies are often eaten by the larvae of dermestids thus supplying an essential nutritional element.*

135

THRIPS

'Thrips' is the common name for insects in the order THYSANOPTERA. There are about 4,000 world species and all are small or very small, in fact many are minute, being only about half a millimetre in length and very slender. Little detail can be seen with the naked eye. However what they lack in size they more than make up for in numbers, some species occurring in certain seasons and localities in extremely large swarms. They invade buildings in great numbers and penetrate into minute cracks and crevices. In this regard they are best known for their habit of secreting themselves between picture frames and backing paper where it is not adhering and thus they make their way between the glass and the mount or picture. Here they die and remain as a small black streak often with a surrounding stain, and an eyesore until the picture is remounted.

In addition, however, they cause small marks between the leaves of books. These are their dead bodies and can be removed by careful brushing but in damp conditions a small brown stain may remain. Other than the presence of their dead bodies they cause no further injury.

Apart from their small size and characteristic slender shape, Thrips may be identified by their rasping and piercing asymetrical mouthparts and the curious bladder-like distensions under the tarsal claws. Not all species possess wings but when present they are ribbon-like and are conspicuously fringed. A habit often observed is the curling upwards of the end of the abdomen when the wings are drawn through the abdominal bristles before flight.

SPIDERS

There is a widespread belief that spiders in buildings play a beneficial role. They prey on insects such as flies, clothes moths and other flying insects which make life difficult for human beings. Generally I think this is true. I would not dream of harming a spider found within my own home, even though my own book collection is extensive and of great importance to me. But in a library or store where ancient manuscripts and antiquarian books are maintained and preserved, spiders – I regret to say – must stay away.

Their dead bodies, as well as live ones on which they prey, serve to nourish the insect enemies of books.

INSECT INTRUDERS

Many insect species in a wide range of orders, make their way into buildings including those where books are displayed and stored. Some are fortuitous wanderers, they enter a building accidentally. They may fly in through the window or may crawl in under the door. Most are not directly harmful to books. Some species enter a building by design in that they are seeking a location for hibernation where they will gain protection from bad weather and from disturbance. A building takes the place of a cave, loose pile of rocks or a hollow tree.

In Britain examples of hibernators are Small Tortoiseshell Butterfly which often spend the winter in the folds of the curtains; The Lacewing, *Chrysopa* in the order NEUROPTERA, a beneficial insect whose larvae consume large numbers of aphids; queen wasps again often use curtains folds as a convenient hibernaculum.

137

CHAPTER ELEVEN

ACARINA

Mites and
Pseudoscorpiones
(False Scorpions)

Mites are not insects but belong to the class ARACHNIDA – the spider group. They are however often associated with insects in various ways and are often described in general accounts involving insects and we do so here. Mites are classified in the sub-class ACARI. They are not only numerous as a species, over 17,000 having already been described with the numbers being frequently added to but they are exceptionally abundant especially in soil and forest litter. In addition they are widely distributed and probably occupy a wider range of habitat than do insects. They are usually very small and this, together with a number of problems of classification have probably contributed to their unpopularity as subjects for study.

The body of mites is not differentiated into two or more distinct regions and unlike the Spiders there is no constriction or waist. There are two pairs of appendages situated around the mouth. In front there are the small 'chelicerae' (but large in spiders') and behind the pedipalps are large and usually conspicuous. Segmentation of the body is usually suppressed.

The life cycle usually commences with the egg stage followed by a six-legged larva, two nymphal stages and finally an eight-legged adult. The life cycle of many species however is complex or may appear to be exceptionally simple.

HOUSE MITE
or
FURNITURE MITE

Latin: *Glycyphagus domesticus* (De Geer.)
American: *Furniture mite*

The male varies from 0.32 to 0.40mm and the female from 0.40 to 0.75mm in length and is whitish or greyish-white in colour. It has a somewhat hexagonal appearance. The legs are long and fairly slender and situated at the hinder end of the female there is a short tube-like organ. The setae on the upperside are long and somewhat feather-like.

This is a widely-distributed mite and although it ranks half a page in Mallis (1969) it is difficult to assess its importance in North America. It would be safe to assume that it is abundant throughout the temperate zones. If this is not so then other closely-related species would assuredly have taken its place.

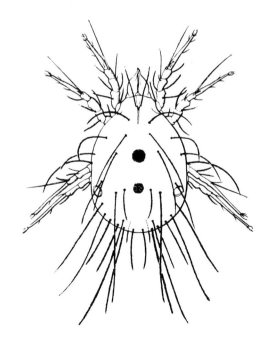

Furniture Mite or House Mite
Glycyphagus domesticus.
Dorsal view of the female.
Length from 0.4 to 0.75mm.

139

The Furniture mite subsists on the superficial fungal flora growing on a wide variety of materials of the household. Their presence therefore is a signal that the environmental conditions are unsatisfactory for human beings, the humidity is too high. Under dry, well-ventilated conditions they would never be observed. No account of this mite would be complete without mention of the upholstery material known as Algerian fibre. In the past it has certainly supported vast numbers of this mite but if dry conditions prevail the mite cannot be a pest. If dampness is allowed to continue then such quantities of the mite are produced that they invade all parts of the building including books. They will however not damage books but will quickly accelerate the fungal environment causing the handling of such books to become disagreeable.

Life-Cycle

The eggs hatch in about 5 days into a six-legged wrinkled larva. It feeds for about 2 days when it becomes swollen and shining in appearance. After resting for a further 2 days it moults into a stage known as a protonymph. It feeds for 4 days rests for a further 2 days and moults again. The resulting stage is known as a deutonymph and lasts for 5 days spent in activity. The final moult produces the 8-legged adult stage. If however, adverse conditions are met a special stage known as the hypopus is assumed enabling the mite to resist desiccating conditions. It is devoid of appendages, is cyst-like and enclosed within the skin of the protonymph. It may remain as a hypopus for as long as six months before changing into an adult when conditions become humid.

GRAIN ITCH MITE

Latin: *Pyemotes (Pediculoides) ventricosus* (Newport.)

American: *Straw itch mite*

This mite is placed in the family TARSONEMIDAE. It is a parasite usually on the larval stage of a large number of insect species. It is usually considered to be beneficial as it reduces the numbers of several pest species best-known being the *Angoumis* grain moth. When cargoes of grain are being moved the mites often transfer their attentions to the dock workers. It is also an important parasite of woodworm – the larvae of *Anobium punctatum* – in Europe. This is its importance to libraries. The female mite buries its head into the soft-skinned insect larva and sucks its juices until only the shrivelled skin remains. The insect larva may carry one or several mites which increase very much in size until they are plainly visible as glistening pearl-like spheres nearly 2mm in diameter.

11.2
Pyemotes ventricosus. *Freshly emerged from abdomen of female (no egg stage). Left: Male never leaves surface of body of parent. Right: Female after mating crawls off to find a host.*

 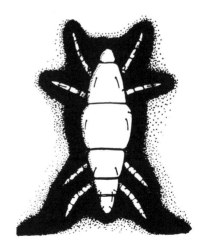

Life Cycle

The life-cycle is unusual and may take as little as 6 days. Up to 50 eggs are produced daily the total number being about 270. The whole of the development of the mite takes place within the body of the female mite so that the adult females and males are produced both of which are active. Fertilisation of the females takes place immediately they are produced. Males only leave the surface of their mother's abdomen when they die. The young adults are active, the males moving over their mother's abdomen whilst the young fertilized females drop off to seek a host insect larva. If a host is not found within a day they die.

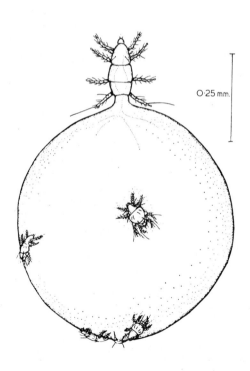

0·25 mm.

11.3
Grain Itch-Mite Pyemotes *ventricosus. A parasite of the larvae of many insect species including some injurious to books but is known to turn its attention to Man causing a severe itching.*

CLOVER or GOOSEBERRY MITE or RED SPIDER

Latin: *Bryobia praetiosa* (Koch)

This mite is classified in the family TETRANYCHIDAE which contains a number of species which are horticultural pests. The body is oval in shape and varies in colour from yellowish-green to bright red. The female measures approximately 0.7mm in length and although all the legs are long and slender, the first pair are by far the longest. There are two interesting minute features (only visible with the aid of a microscope): the back bears a number of club-shaped setae and the claw of the first pair of legs is extraordinarily complex.

The eggs are globular in shape and bright red and the young larvae which are also bright red feed on plant sap. A wide range of host plants have been recorded from fruit trees to grass species and clover.

The importance of this mite as a pest lies in its migratory habit and the extraordinary numbers which occur during favourable weather conditions. This is usually in Spring, in the South of England swarms enter buildings from the end of April to the beginning of May and occasionally in the Autumn. The species is parthenogenetic and all the mites found in buildings are ovigerous and are seeking egg-laying sites which approximate to such situations as under loose bark crevices. Thus they are laid on rough brickwork under loose wallpaper and similar.

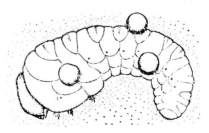

Three mites of Pediculoides ventricosus *infesting larva of* Anobium punctatum.

143

Life Cycle

In the New York area this is mid-January until early Summer but they occur in smaller proportions or live on in hibernation throughout the winter indoors. There are two reasons why this species is a potential pest in libraries apart from the undesirability of experiencing large numbers of mites crawliung around. Firstly, when the body of a mite is squashed a small red stain remains which is conspicuous on paper. Secondly, the dead bodies may serve as protein food supply for dermestid larvae.

In North America the Gooseberry mite was of little importance as a pest species until about 1950 but it is now a serious invader of buildings. Some investigators believe that it is not a single species but rather a complex of forms but little differentiated from each other. This is the best place to refer to environmental control. In the U.S.A. it is recommended that a grass-free area in the form of a band up to one metre in width is left around the building. This is an effective barrier.

Red Spider Mite Dorsal view of female. Length 0.7mm.
Reproduced by permission of the Trustees of the British Museum.

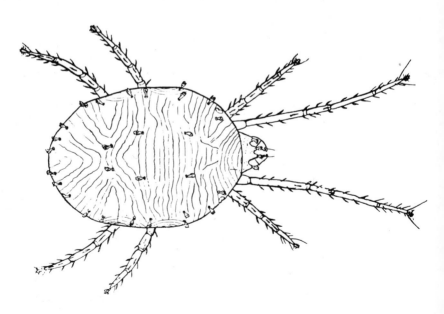

PSEUDO SCORPIONES

False Scorpions,
Book Scorpions

False-scorpions constitute another order of the ARACHNIDA known as the PSEUDOSCORPIONES quite separate from true scorpions to which they show a superficial likeness. At least the pedipalps are enlarged and scorpion-like but there is no narrow tail or metasoma, and a sting is absent. In addition all false scorpions are small, the largest being only about 7mm in length. There are about 1,600 species known, distributed worldwide and they are usually coloured in browns and greys.

The Book-scorpion, *Cheiridium museorum*, has been known for a long time as a denizen of books. Aristotle (384BC-322BC) was familiar with it for he wrote 'In books other small animals are found, some of which are like scorpions without tails'. Robert Hooke, gave an illustration of what is thought to have been this species in his book 'Micrographia' in 1664. Two other species of false-scorpions are also known to live in habitations, *Chelifer cancroides* and *Allochernes italicus* and all three species are more likely to be found in old food warehouses. However, none of these species harms books as they are entirely carnivorous. They lie in wait for a small creature to come along and then pounce upon it and grip it in the pedipalps. The prey is likely to be silverfish, psocids, small flies or mites. The book-scorpion can exist in a dry environment.

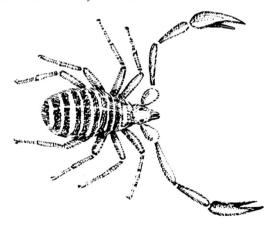

Book-scorpion.

145

CHAPTER TWELVE

OPTIMUM BOOK STORAGE CONDITIONS

The Environment for Books
Insects as Indicators of Damp
Prevention of Insect Attack

The optimum climatic conditions for book and document storage have been tested over a number of years and are applicable over a wide range of book types both with regard to materials and make-up. Both temperature and Relative Humidity must be constant. Temperature should lie between 13°C and 18°C (55°F-65°F) and Relative Humidity between fifty-five and sixty-five per cent. There must be adequate ventilation amounting to six complete air changes an hour. Relative Humidity and Rate of air change are closely linked. The problem in a library is to ensure that rate of air change and thus Relative Humidity applies to all parts of the book storage area. Most libraries find it most convenient to stack and display books against the walls. This is the most efficient use of book display space if no book conservation factors were being considered. In fact, the small space between the books and the wall is an area of stagnant air usually of high Relative Humidity. Librarians are often surprised to find, in a room of otherwise well-night perfect climatic conditions that a book withdrawn from such a shelf, that moulds are apparent and sometimes the associated fauna such as book-lice.

The ideal situation is one where all books are accommodated in island sites, i.e. no books displayed against walls. If this is not possible then the space between the books and the walls should be increased to as wide as possible and tests made to ensure that the air is being moved at the recommended rate.

In some parts of the world, notably in North America, air conditioning in buildings is common place. Nevertheless the 'microclimate' of stagnant areas must be under constant surveillance, especially as the hazard is likely to be both higher temperatures and much higher Relative Humidities.

One important tool of the librarian used to reduce the Relative Humidity in these special 'micro-areas' is the De-humidifier. This is a heat-pump adapted for domestic and light commercial use. It is designed to extract excess moisture from walls and the surrounding atmosphere. The Dryer draws moisture-laden air over a cooling coil which condenses the water vapour and the water is collected in a container removed from time to time as necessary. The cold air blown through the hot coil, cooling the machine and re-circulating warm, dry air to the general atmosphere. Maximum water extraction is up to 15 litres per 24 hours and some models can be moved around.

Condensation is another source of moisture which must be eliminated. This is where warm moisture-laden air comes into close proximity with a cool surface such as metal and liquid water is deposited upon it.

Clean Air

The air being used for ventilation where books are stored must be clean. At certain seasons according to geographical location, the air supports relatively large quantities of minute organisms such as pollen, fungal spores, seeds and small insects such as thrips and aphids. From time to time extraordinary numbers of insects are recorded, especially in, but not entirely confined to, tropical areas. The swarming insects are often attracted to light at night and enter the room if windows are left open.

Quite apart from the use of air-conditioning equipment, many designs of which will ensure that organisms and dust are precluded, equipment is available which can be sited almost anywhere within a room which can be reached by an electric cable. A fan draws air into the unit where, an electric charge is imparted to all the extraneous particles. These are then drawn magneticaly onto collection cells. Odours are removed by activated charcoal. A fringe benefit of some economic significance is that the redecorating of the rooms can be delayed for several years before it becomes necessary.

New Flooring

It follows from what has been stated above that when a new building is being designed or an old one being refurbished for the purpose of book display or storage that the type and design of flooring is of the utmost importance. The surface must be completely plane with no cracks to allow trapping of possible insect foodstuff and insect harbourage and any angles with the vertical walls likewise. It is now some years since the food manufacturing industry, beset with similar problems pioneered, this simple approach to insect pest prevention. Plastic angle contour to bridge the gap between horizontal floors and vertical walls is now widely distributed.

Pets and Plants

Two other aspects of biological infiltration into libraries must not be overlooked. Pets such as cats and dogs and ornamental pot plants might appear innocuous enough, certainly in most homes. Unfortunately they must not be tolerated in buildings housing book collections. This is not because of any damage they might cause to books directly but on account of ecto-parasites which they carry, hair which they shed and the possibility of secretions and excretions. All this extraneous material might help to nourish the larvae of ptinid, dermestid and anobiid beetles. Indeed in some species nutrients essential for complete development might be supplied from this source.

The important point about all insects occurring in Libraries or wherever books are stored, is that they must be eliminated by some means. In the most sophisticated situations this may be accomplished by denying access to the building by insects through strict air conditioning arrangements. Windows must not be opened to the exterior unless wandering insects are thereby trapped. Access through doors must be regulated by some means, double doors etc.

The reason for this is that a number of the insects die during hibernation and thus their bodies or remains of them are available to those insects, or more usually their larvae, which cause damage to books directly. The protein in insect bodies is often of the greater importance in their nutrition. In some cases indeed, it would appear to be essential for the complete development to the adult stage of many insects otherwise subsisting on the materials of which books are constructed.

The destruction of insect collections by book-damaging insects – e.g. dermestids and psocids – has been widely recorded. They are also often stated to be found around spiders' webs and other places where dead insects ocur. It is to be regretted that otherwise beneficial insects such as Small Tortoiseshell Butterfly and the Lacewing must be controlled, but this is in the interests of book conservation. Besides hibernators, of course, insect intruders in other categories find their way into buildings. Large numbers of insects such as moths, but other insect groups besides, are attracted to light and may enter buildings at night through open windows and doors. Often such invasions are on a large scale and again constitute a hazard to books indirectly.

A number of bird species habitually nest in buildings and several others do so less commonly. In Britain, the jackdaw, house sparrow, feral pigeon, house martin, swift and starling belong to the first category and a longer list makes up the second. Birds' nests are the natural habit of the immature stages of dermestid beetles where the larvae feed on feathers, wool, hair, dried carrion, dead fledglings and faecal matter. From this situation the larvae wander into the buildings and are attracted to warmth. Their route has been traced along hot water systems into airing cupboards and woollen blanket stores where they cause much damage. It is certain that they could enter areas where books are stored by the same route. It is regrettable from the bird conservation point of view but possible bird nest sites in library buildings must be denied to them. It is preferable to survey a building and render it unattractive to nesting birds rather than to remove nests already constructed. It is an undeniable fact that birds' nests are a source of dermestid larvae which constitute a serious hazard to leather-bound books.

Food must never be consumed in libraries and regulations should be strictly enforced to ensure that this never happens. Food crumbs dropping onto the floor and lodging into cracks between floorboards, and other inaccessible crannies, are well known as nourishment for the larvae of the Brown House Moth and Spider Beetles, both important insect pests of books and known to spend their larval life amongst the indeterminate fluff and debris to be found in such places.

In some libraries or buildings where libraries are located, canteens or restaurants are included. This is not a good arrangement as kitchens bring in a number of additional insect species creating hazards to books.

Indicators of Damp

There remains one other group of arthropods to be considered. It is a varied assemblage some of which are insects and some are not. However they share a character in that they are to be found in damp or very damp sitautinos and they generally shun the light. In areas of high rainfall they are usually more abundant. In buildings they are more likely to be found in kitchens and washrooms especially where there are water leaks, permanent damp areas or where damp cloths are allowed to stay about in dark corners. Sometimes they are found wandering at some distance from their normal habitat.

The presence of these arthropods is a firm indication that the location is too damp for book storage and should be remedied immediately.

COLLEMBOLA
Springtails

These small primitive wingless insects never exceed 6mm in length. They are very numerous in nature and act as scavengers in the soil, amongst dead leaves and other vegetable detritus. They are found in Europe and North America. As indoor pests they are seldom serious, but some species are nevertheless often found in damp, dark situations. When disturbed they may jump several inches into the air, probably in an effort to evade the attentions of predatory animals. They are certainly very successful in becoming invisible very quickly after two or three jumps. If a bucket is moved suddenly Springtails are often seen jumping themselves into a new position. Jumping is brought about by a stout, forked tail which bends under the abdomen and is there held in position until released by a small organ on the third abdominal segment. When it springs backwards the tail propels the light, fragile insect into the air.

The anatomy of Springtails is remarkable in that the antennae are composed of only four segments and there are only six segments in the abdomen, which is the smallest number found in any insect.

Collembola do not undergo a larval or pupal stage, the young Springtails being similar to the parent in shape when they hatch from the egg. Springtails require a very high atmospheric humidity and shun light. The different species show preference for different foodstuffs but most seem to subsist on vegetable and animal debris and occasionally on living plants, but very little economic damage is caused. Wherever they are found the environment is too damp for the safe storage of books.

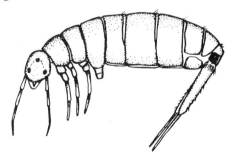

A Springtail Collembola

WOOD LICE

Woodlice are crustaceans classified in the order ISOPODA. In North America closely related species are widespread and are commonly known as Sowbugs and Pillbugs. Unlike the great majority of the CRUSTACEA they are terrestrial and the great hazard to their survival is desiccation. They feed on heavily decayed wood and other soft vegetable debris and they will chew up damp paper and their faecal pellets are often scattered about.

Three well-known and common British species are:

Oniscus asellus up to 15mm in length and 7.5mm in width. The integument is slightly shiny and the colour is slaty grey with irregular lighter markings. It is one of the largest and commonest of the British wood lice.

Porcellio scaber is 17mm long. The integument is covered with tubercles which gives it a matt appearance and this character serves to distinguish it from *Oniscus asellus.*

Armadillidium vulgare: this is another large wood louse growing up to 18mm in length and is a little more than twice as long as broad. In colour it is rather variable and although usualy of a light grey shade, black or yellow individuals may be observed. This species is often called the pill wood louse on account of its ability to roll up into a ball on being disturbed. It requires a chalky diet and is usually only common in chalky or limestone districts.

Wood Louse Oniscus asellus. *An isopod Crustacean up to 15mm in length, slaty grey in colour. Found only in extremely damp conditions where books would be totally destroyed.*

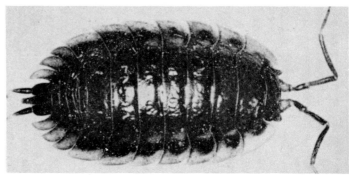

152

THE PLASTER AND FUNGUS BEETLE

The following six beetle species found in houses in Britain are known as 'Plaster' and 'Fungus' beetles. This is because they are usually present in a house shortly after its erection when the plastering is new and still very damp. In such conditions surface-growing moulds and mildews occur on plaster, paper and wood and it is on these fungi that the larvae and the adult Plaster Beetles subsist.

Two families of beetles are involved and the commonest species likely to be found in houses are as follows:

CRYPTOPHAGIDAE	LATHRIDIIDAE
(Fungus Beetles)	(Plaster Beetles)
Cryptophagus acutangulus	*Aridius nodifer*
Cryptophagus cellaris	*Thes bergrothi*
Cryptophagus distinguendus	*Lathridius minutus*

Their presence is an indication that conditions are too damp for the storage of books.

There are 80 species of CRYPTOPHAGIDAE found in Britain and of these *Cryptophagus cellaris* is probably the most widely distributed, but it is found in mills, warehouses and large damp cellars more often than in dwellings. *Cryptophagus acutangulus*, however, is more common in the latter type of premises. In the LATHRIDIIDAE there are 48 British species of which the three species noted above most commonly occur in households.

What is known concerning the detailed biology of the various species of Plaster Beetles shows no significant differences so that they are dealt with in this account as a group.

Appearance

All Plaster Beetles are small, mostly within the length of 1.0 to 2.5mm. In both families the antennae are clubbed; the club consisting of three segments. Those species in the CRYPTOPHAGIDAE are characterized by the shape of the pronotum which is thickened at the front and bears a tooth

153

at the centre of each side. The greatest width of the pronotum is approximately equal to the width of the wing cases

In the LATHRIDIIDAE, on the other hand, the width of the pronotum is often much less than the width of the wing cases, and a feature common to the three species being considered in this account, is the strong longitudinal ridging of the wing cases or rows of deep pits. In the species *Aridius nodifer* the ridging extends to the pronotum. Plaster Beetles are dark in colour, varying from reddish-brown to black.

In North America several species of the genus *Cartodere* in the family LATHRIDIIDAE occur and are similar in habit. As in the British species when rooms are dried out the insects disappear.

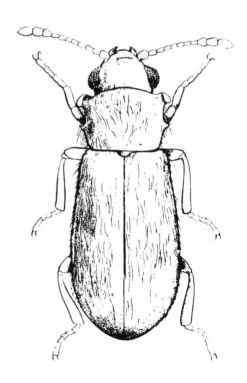

The Fungus Beetle
Cryptophagus acutangulus.

154

CURCULIONIDAE

Weevils

The weevil family, CURCULIONIDAE, is the largest family in number of species in the whole of the animal kingdom. It has been estimated that there are about 200,000 of them. The adults are characterized by the head being prolonged into a rostrum which carries the antennae, the latter being conspicuously elbowed. The wing cases are usually fused and the wings are functionless or absent. The larvae are legless.

Relatively few species are found in buildings but when they occur are usually indicative of very damp and unventilated conditions. One species *Euophyrum confine* has become of considerable importance through damaging damp woodwork in basements and similar situations. This species originated in New Zealand and although it was not recorded until 1937 it is now established as a house pest in the southern half of England.

Another species, *Pentarthrum huttoni*, is very similar both in appearance and habits to the New Zealand species but has been known for much longer although it has not become so abundant as *E. confine*. Both species are dark brown to pitchy-black in colour.

Instances are known of book damage by both species. The weevil *Rhyncolus culinaris*, is recorded as injuring books by Petrova (1953) in Moscow. Weevils do not appear to be a hazard to well-stored books.

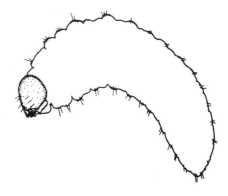

Larva of Euophyrum confine.
Note absence of legs.

155

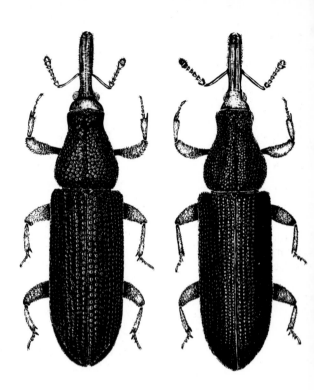

Left: Euophyrum confine.
Length 3.8mm.
Right: Pentarthrum huttoni.
Length 4.0mm.

CHAPTER THIRTEEN
CONTROL AND ELIMINATION OF INSECT PESTS OF BOOKS

CONTROL MEASURES

Control of the insect pests in books can be split into separate parts. Firstly control of the book-injuring insects in the actual books themselves and secondly control of the pests in the immediate environment in which the books are located.

Extermination of Injurious Insects in Books

Books from a recent acquisition should be thoroughly examined in a separate room in which no other books are stored. This should be considered as quarantine. The examination should be carried out with great care page by page and each page carefully brushed with a clean, dry, soft brush in order to remove dust and miscellaneous debris as well as any insects that may be present. The books should be subjected to a recommended disinfestation process such as the Yale University Deep-freeze technique or fumigation (for other than old books or leather-bound books). Only then should the books take their place in the general library shelves.

DISINFESTATION OF THE BOOK ENVIRONMENT

It is an historical fact that collections of old books have usually been housed in old buildings, certainly in Europe. Many books show the scars of consequent insect damage. Let us then look at the immediate book environment in an old building.

FLOORS

Perhaps the most unsatisfactory feature concerns the floors. These would be wooden, of floor-boards and would have been a tight fit when the building was unheated but which with some measure of heating in more recent years there would be a 3mm gap between the boards. The wooden skirting boards (kickboards) similarly would show about a 5mm gap. Within these ample crevices the fluff and debris of half a century has accumulated, periodically wetted perhaps when scrubbed or mopped. These are the optimum conditions in Europe for the Brown House moth and the Spider beetles. Unless the floor boards are removed and replaced there is no alternative but to scrape out the debris and fill with a non-contracting sealant.

In libraries there must be no floor coverings of any description. Carpets or plastic coverings would not only constitute a cover-up operation for what has gone before but would provide the ideal conditions for Silverfish and other bristle-tails for hiding during daylight hours. As mentioned previously, these are areas with a low rate of air flow and likely to be of high Relative Humidity.

FUMIGATION

Fumigation is the application of a toxic substance (in our case toxic to insects) in the form of a gas, vapour, volatile liquid or solid in the atmosphere of a closed container. The latter may be a fumigation chamber or a stack covered with gas-proof sheets such as specially-manufactured PVC-covered tarpaulins, or a complete structure such as a building similarly covered.

It might be thought that tarpaulins, rolled and clipped together would not be efficient but, in fact, experienced operators are able to carry out this covering making the joins sufficiently gas-tight for the purpose.

The required concentration of the gas must be maintained for a specified period. The product of the fumigant concentration and the length of time for which it is held is known as the CT product. Because of the higher metabolic rate and respiratory activity of insects at higher temperatures the dosage of fumigant is reduced. At the end of the fumigation period the tarpaulins are removed and stacked windows opened and ventilating fans kept running where dead-air pockets are likely, until all the gas is removed.

158

For some gases, odour is sufficient to tell when it has been removed (or rather the lack of it). Special detectors are available for some fumigants. It must be borne in mind that fumigants do not impart any residual properties. When the fumigant has been dispersed reinfestation can take place if the surrounding environment carries a reservoir of the infesting insects.

The decision to use fumigant must not be taken lightly. No fumigant should be used without the appropriate safety equipment and without training or previous experience in fumigation techniques. For an illustrated account of fumigation of buildings see Hickin (1971).

The choice of fumigants is limited. Neither Methyl Bromide nor Ethylene Oxide should be used on leather-bound books on account of some leathers being made brittle. Although the use of chloroform is described by Baynes-Cope (1981) in the case of single books if not too large. The book is stood up fanwise in a container which can be closed and sealed together with a small jar containing the chloroform at the rate of 15ml per cubic metre of the container. The container is sealed and left for ten days. It is then opened out of doors. If a large number of books are to be fumigated a professional firm should be consulted.

Fumigation however is not now recommended for old books now that the new deep-freeze technique has been established.

DISINFESTATION OF BOOKS BY DEEP-FREEZE TECHNIQUE

Since 1977 Yale University Library have employed a new method of eliminating insects from books. It was first used on a section of the Beineoke Rare Book and Manuscript Library comprising 37,000 books. Only a small number of the books were found to be harbouring book-harming insects, but all were subjected to the treatment as a precautionary treatment.

The books were first sealed in polyethylene bags and were then placed in a blast freezer chamber at a temperature of $-30°C$ ($-20°F$) for a period of three days. When returned to room temperature they were replaced in the shelves. The blast freezer chamber was constructed in the lower basement level and was 10 feet by 10 feet (3m by 3m) square and special steel trucks were used to wheel 300-400 books at a time into the chamber. After treatment the books are returned to the standard library conditions at Yale of 70°F and 50 per cent Relative Humidity.

The great advantages of this method are that no toxic materials are employed and thus no possible danger to staff and others who use the library. No danger of chemical reaction of the fumigant with the constituent materials of the book. The least possible interruption in the smooth running of the library system. This process is a regular and permanent part of the library's treatment of all books acquired.

BOOKCASES AND SHELVING OF WOOD

One of the most important tasks for those responsible for the care and well-being of books is to ensure that the shelves and room furniture in which the books are housed do not contribute to their infestation and injury by wood-boring insects. In tropical and subtropical areas termites are the main hazard but in temperate regions their place as wood-destroyers is taken by beetles (COLEOPTERA) of several families. Chief among these in Britain is the ANOBIIDAE. Elsewhere in Europe much depends on the timber species concerned. Soft woods (timber of coniferous species) are often heavily tunnelled by the larvae of the Longhorn beetle in the family CERAMBY-CIDAE.

Bookcases and shelving of wood must be chemically treated so as to exterminate all immature stages of wood-boring beetles within the wood and to prevent re-infestaion for a number of years in the future. The most important species is *Anobium punctatum* the Common woodworm. Woodworm showing a present or past attack can be identified by

160

numbers of small circular flight holes between 1 and 2mm in diameter.

TREATMENT

Bookcases and wooden shelving should be examined carefully and dust removed together with any debris which has accumulated in corners (the latter should be scraped out with a pointed knife).

Two wetting coats of a special insecticidal fluid should be applied over all wooden surfaces (top and bottom). This may be applied by spray or brush but better control is generally obtained by the use of the latter. Care must be taken not to apply excess fluid especially where the woodwork is tunnelled extensively and so soaking up the fluid and taking longer to dry.

The Special Insecticidal fluid is quick-drying and of minimum odour and consists of Lindane in a refined oil solvent with additives to enhance solubility. The drying time depends on the dimensions and species of the wood but should not be less than three days. In view of the variables it would be recommended to test dryness with a sheet of newspaper pressed against the treated wood for two days in order to observe whether any 'oiliness' has seeped out. In any event for the super cautious the shelves could be lined with paper before the books are replaced and removed after a prolonged period of time depending on the circumstances.

GENERAL WOODEN STRUCTURES

It follows from what has been stated above that all wooden furniture and indeed structural timber, wooden flooring etc. should be included in any programme of reducing or exterminating possible book-damaging pests whereas the treatment of items of furniture may fall within the capabilities of library conservationists whose responsibilities fall within the category of books and their immediate housing, the conservation of the general structure is in another and entirely separate category indeed in most cases the

161

treatment of the timber components of a building is usually entrusted to a specialist preservation company under contract.

Important reasons for such a decision are: Agreed safety procedures must operate when toxic chemicals are in use in buildings in the interests of both the users of the building and the technicians carrying out the treatment; A number of the treatment processes require high standards of expertise, much experience and special fire precautions. In most countries these are regulated by law, codes of practice or voluntary agreements.

CONTROL AND PREVENTION OF SUBTERRANEAN TERMITE DAMAGE

Probably the most efficaceous method of achieving success in not only controlling an existing infestation, but to prevent such a happening for some years in the future, is known as Soil Treatment. Briefly this consists of applying insecticidal fluids to the immediate environment of the building so that termite colonies are unable to sustain themselves in such conditions. In new buildings by far the best is to treat the soil of the site before actual building operations take place or rather after foundations and service trenches have been excavated but before any cement has been 'poured' into foundations or slab.

The early insecticides used, such as DDT Dieldrin etc., were found to give excellent results but had a pollutant effect on wildlife in some cases far removed from the point of application. The specific insecticides used are now under control by national agencies together with the precise methods to be followed and safety regulations to be adopted. Because of the high technical standards to be attained it would appear that this would generally be achieved by utilizing the services of a Pest Control Company under contract. An outline of the process with illustrations and diagrams is given by Hickin (1971).

PREVENTION OF TERMITE ATTACK

This subject can be divided into, firstly, the prevention of termite attack of books and secondly the prevention of termite attack of the immediate book environment.

PRESSURE IMPREGNATION

Taking the second part first, all wood can be treated to render it immune to termite attack by application of chemical substances. In buildings the most widely used process employs formulation of copper and chrome arsenates which are water soluble and which are applied by various pressure impregnation processes. A feature of these methods is the substantial degree of fixation of the chemical substances which occurs with the wood substance which renders the formulation insoluble in water. The termiticidal effect of the CCA preservatives is conferred by the copper and arsenic the chromium playing an important part in effecting the permanence.

As well as preventing attack by termites such processes render the treated timber immune to wood-boring beetles. Most major cities throughout the world possess facilities for Pressure impregnation of timber.

BIBLIOGRAPHY and AUTHOR INDEX

ADAMS, R. G. (1978). First British Infestation of *Reesa vespulae* (Milliron) (COLEOPTERA = DERMESTIDAE, *Entomologists Gazette. 29:* 73-75.

ANONYMOUS (1904). Psocids, book lice, dust lice, etc. British Museum (Natural History) *Econ. Leaflet* No. 4.

ANONYMOUS (1978). New Technique kills insects Harmful to Books. *AB Bookman's Weekly*. Jan. 1978: 158-160.

ANONYMOUS (1984). Freeze drying saves stock of valuable books. *Laboratory Equipment Digest*. Sept. 1984, p. 13.

ARAI, H. and MORI, H. (1975). Biodeterioration of Books and their Pest Control in Japan. Sei. for Conserv. No. 14: 33-43.

AUSTEN, E. E., McKENNY HUGHES, A. W. and STRINGER, H. (1935). *Clothes Moths and House Moths*. British Museum and Natural History Economy Series 14.

BACK, E. A. and COTTON, R. T. (1930). Insect Pests of Upholstered Furniture, *Jour. Econ. Ent.* 23: 833-7.

BACK, E. A. and COTTON, R. T. (1936). The Furniture Carpet Beetle (*Anthrenus vorax* Waterh.) a pest of increasing importance in the United States. *Proc. Entom. Soc. Wash.*, 38: 191-198.

BACK, E. A. and COTTON, R. T. (1938). The Black Carpet Beetle, *Attagenus piceus* (Oliv.), *Jour. Econ. Ent.*, 31: 280-6.

BACK, E. A. (1939). *Bookworms. Smiths, Inst. Ann. Rept.* 365-74.

BACK, E. A. (1939). A new pest of books, *Neogastrallus librinocens* Fisher. *Jour. Econ. Ent.*, 32: 642-645.

BACK, E. A. (1945). Minutes of the 553rd regular meeting of the Entomological Society of Washington. *Proc. Ent. Soc. Wash.* 47(6): 182-184.

BANSA, H. (1981). The conservation of Library collections in tropical and sub-tropical conditions. The problems of the increased dangers of damage and decay in areas of high temperature and humidity. *IFLA Journal*, 7(3): 264-267.

BANYSHNIKOVA, Z. P. (1970). Some Observations of the Development and Nutrition of Booklice. *Restaurator*, I: 199-212.

BAYNES-COPE, A. D. (1981). *Caring for Books and Documents*. British Museum Publications.

BROADHEAD, E. and HOBBY, B. M. (1944). Studies on a Species of *Liposcelis* (CORRODENTIA, LIPOSCELIDAE) Occurring in Stored Products in Britain. Part I *Ent. Mon. Mag.*, 80: 45-59. Part II. *Ent. Mon. Mag.*, 80: 163-173.

BUSVINE, J. (1951 and later). Editions. *Insects and Hygiene*. Methuen, London.

CHANDEL, A. S. and DEVENDER, K. (1981). Preservation of Reading Materials in Libraries: A Practical Approach. *Lucknow Librarian* 13(1): 21-26.

CLOUDESLEY-THOMPSON, J. L. (1958). *Spiders, Scorpions, Centipedes* and *Mites*. Pergamon.

CORNWELL, P. B. (1968). *The Cockroach*, Vol. 1, Hutchinson, London.

CORNWELL, P. B. (1973). *Pest Control in Buildings*, Hutchinson, London.

CUNHA, G. M. and CUNHA, D. G. (1983). Library and Archives Conservation. Scarecrow Press. 2 vols.

CYMOREK, S. (1977). Schadinsekten in Buchern. Wolfenbütteler. Forschungen I: 33-59.

CYMOREK, S. (1962). Uber das Paarungsverhalten und zur Biologie des Holzschadlings *Ptilinus pectinicornis* L. (COLEOPTERA ANOBIIDAE). Verh. X1. Internat. Kongr. Entomol., Wien 1960, Bd. 11: 335-339.

CYMOREK, S. (1972). *Nicobium castaneum* W. (COL. ANOBIIDAE), A pest in wood materials and works of art. Proc. 2. Int. Biodeterior Symp. (Lunteren 1971), Biodeterior Materials 2: 408-415.

CYMOREK, S. (1975). On the species problem in *Nicobium castaneum* (COL. ANOBIIDAE). J. Inst. Wood Sci. 7/2 (38): 58-59.

DELANEY, M. J. (1954). Handbooks for the Identification of British Insects. Vol. 1 part 2. Roy. Ent. Soc. Lond.

DOHRING, E. (1970). Zur Biologie und Bekampfung des messingkafers (Niptus hololeucus Fald). Der praktische Schadlingsbekampfer. 22(3): 29-35.

DVORYASHINA, Z. P. (1979). Some Regularities of Book Storage Contamination by Insects. Restaurator 3: 109-116.

EDMUNDS, L. R. (1957). Observations on the biology and life history of the Brown Cockroach, *Periplaneta brunnea* Burmeister. *Proc. Ent. Soc. Wash.* 59: 283-286.

EDWARDS, R. (1969). *Anthrenus sarnicus* Mroczk. (Col., DERMESTIDAE). The Present Status of this Insect in the British Isles. *Ent. Mon. Mag.* 105: 119-121.

GHANI, M. A. and SWEETMAN, H. L. (1951). Ecological studies of the book louse, *Liposcelis divinatorius* (Mull.). *Ecology* 32: 230-244.

GILLEDGE, C. J. (1929). The Insect Pests of Books. An annotated bibliography. *Library association Rc.* (2) vol. 7. 240-242.

HADLINGTON, P. (1962). Pests of Australian Homes and Industry. New South Wales University Press.

HAINES, F. H. (1932). *Borkhausenia pseudospretella* Stt. *Attacking Book-bindings.* Ent. Mon. Mag. 68: 68.

HARRIS, W. V. (1961 and 1972). *Termites, their Recognition and Control.* Longman.

HICKIN, N. E. (1962, 1968 and 1975). *The Insect Factor in Wood Decay.* Hutchinson and Associated Business Programmes (1975). London.

166

HICKIN, N. E. (1971). *Termites a World Problem*. Hutchinson, London.

HINTON, H. E. (1945). A monograph of the Beetles Associated with Stored Products. Vol. 1. Trustees of the British Museum, London.

HOWE, R. W. and BURGES, H. D. (1952). *Studies on beetles of the family PTINIDAE* V1. The biology of *ptinus fur* (4). and *P. sexpunctatus* Panzer, *Bull. Ent. Res.* 42(3): 499-513.

HOWE, R. W. (1957). A Laboratory Study of the Cigarette Beetle *Lasioderma serricorne* F., with a Critical Review of the Literature. *Bull entomol. Res.* 48(1): 9-56.

KLOET, G. S. and HINCKS, W. D. (1945 and later Editions). *A Check List of Britsh Insects*. Published by the Authors, Stockport.

KLOET, G. A. and HINCKS, W. D. (1977). A Check List of British Insects. 2nd Edn. Revised by R. D. Pope pt 3. COLEOPTERA and STEPSIPTERA *R. ent. Soc. London*.

KOESTERER, M. G. and GEATING, J. A. (1976). Application and Utilization of a Space Chamber for the Drying of Books, Documents and other materials and their Decontamination to Prevent Biodeterioration. *Journal of Environmental Sciences* Sept.-Oct. 1976: 29-33.

KOWALIK, R. (1979). Some remarks of a Microbiologist on protection of Library Materials against Insects. *Restauratur* 3(3): 117-122.

LUFF, M. L. (1982). *Reesa vespulae* (Milliron) (COLEOPTERA: DERMESTIDAE) infesting stored Rye inflorescences near Newcastle. *Entomologists Gazette* 33: 40.

MALLIS, A. (1945, fifth edition 1969). *Handbook of Pest Control*. MacNair-Dorland, New York, U.S.A.

NEW, T. R. (1974). Psocoptera – Handbooks for the Identification of British Insects. 4 (pt. 7). *R. ent. Soc., London*.

NIGAN, L. N. (1933). The Life-history of a common Cockroach (Periplaneta americana Linnaeus). *Ind. J. Agric. Sci.* 3: 530-543).

167

OLAFSSON, E. (1979). *Natturufraedingurison* 49 (2-3): 155-162.

PETROVA, L. G. (1953) Editor and BELYAKOVA, L. A. and KOZULINA, O. V. Editors (1958). *Collection of Materials on the Preservation of Library Resources*. U.S.S.R. State Library, Department of Book Preservation and Restoration, Moskva. Translated from the Russian by the Israel, Program for Scientific Translations, Jerusalem.

ROSEWALL, O. W. (1930). The Biology of the Booklouse *Troctes divinatoria* Mull. *Ann. Ent. Soc. Amer.* 23: 192-4.

SCHWENKE, W. (1974). *Die Forstschadlinge Europas* Band 2. Paul Parey. Hamburg and Berlin.

SHUKAI, P. S. (1980). Preservation of Library Materials. *International Library Movement* 2(3): 73-78.

TAKAHASI, S. and UCHIUMI, M. (1934). Studies on *Attagenus piceus* Oliv., a pest of raw silk. First Report. *R.A.E.A.* 23: 209.

TAYLOR, R. L. (1928). A foreign book pest enters Boston. *Jour. Econ. Ent.* 21: 626-627.

THOMSON, G. (1978). *The Museum Environment*. Butterworths, London.

WATSON, J. R. (1943). A tropical book-worm enters Florida. *Neogastrallus librinocens* Fisher. *Fla. Ent.* 26(4): 61-63.

WEIDNER, H. (1971). Bestimmungstabellen der Vorratsschadlinge und des Hausungeziefers Mitteleuropas. Gustav Fischer Verlag. Stuttgart.

WEIS, H. B. and CARRUTHERS, R. H. (11945). Insect Enemies of Books.

INDEX OF SCIENTIFIC (LATIN) NAMES

170

INDEX OF COMMON NAMES IN ENGLISH

INDEX OF AMERICAN NAMES OF BOOK-HARMING ARTHROPODS

INDEX OF FRENCH NAMES OF BOOK-HARMING ARTHROPODS

INDEX OF GERMAN NAMES OF BOOK-HARMING ARTHROPODS

INDEX OF SPANISH NAMES OF BOOK-HARMING ARTHROPODS